BIRDS
OF
VICTORIA
AND VICINITY

**ROBIN BOVEY • WAYNE CAMPBELL
BRYAN GATES
Illustrated by EWA PLUCIENNIK**

LONE
PINE

The Publisher:
Lone Pine Publishing
#206 10426-81 Avenue
Edmonton, Alberta, Canada
T6E 1X5

Canadian Cataloguing in Publication Data

Bovey, Robin B. (Robin Bruce), 1947-
    Birds of Victoria

    ISBN 0-919433-75-8

    1. Birds - British Columbia - Victoria.
2. Bird watching - British Columbia - Victoria.
I. Campbell, Wayne. II. Gates, Bryan R.
III. Pluciennik, Ewa, 1954- IV. Ho, Kitty. V. Title.
QL685.5.B7B693 1989   598.29711'34 C89-091090-1

Cover Design: Ewa Pluciennik
Colour Illustrations: Ewa Pluciennik, Kitty Ho, Joan Johnston
Black and White Illustrations: Donna McKinnon, Ewa Pluciennik
Book Design and Layout: Yuet Chan and Ewa Pluciennik
Typesetting: Michael Hawkins and Phillip Kennedy
Editorial: Mary Walters Riskin
Separations: Scangraphics Ltd.
Printing: Quality Color Press Inc.

Publisher's Acknowledgement
The publisher gratefully acknowledges the assistance of the Federal Department of Communications, Alberta Culture and Multiculturalism, the Canada Council, and the Alberta Foundation for the Literary Arts in the production of this book.

CONTENTS

PREFACE

Most of us have been intrigued by birds at one time or another. For some this interest has evolved into a pastime, but for most of us it is a small facet of our lives that we enjoy when we can.

Many people enjoy feeding birds and having them around the yard. Birdwatching provides us with a tangible contact with nature in an urban existence. This book is for people who enjoy birds, but who don't regard themselves as professional birdwatchers, people who would like to know more, without buying comprehensive field guides and expensive equipment and then trying to decide which birds are actually found in the urban environment. This is a guide for the back yard birdwatcher.

Each bird is illustrated in colour and there are descriptions and illustrations of the habitats within our city which are particularly attractive to birds. At the back of the book there is a section on how to attract birds to the yard. This section deals with feeders, nesting boxes and explains which trees, shrubs and garden settings are most attractive to birds.

ACKNOWLEDGEMENTS

The authors are grateful to the following for their advice, assistance and encouragement in the preparation of this book: Eileen C. Campbell, Sharon Gates, Elizabeth John, Grant Kennedy and Kathie Kennedy.

The Victoria Natural History Society is gratefully acknowledged for authorizing the use of its "Checklist of Birds of Victoria and Southeastern Vancouver Island." The checklist was prepared with assistance from the Public Conservation Assistance Fund of British Columbia.

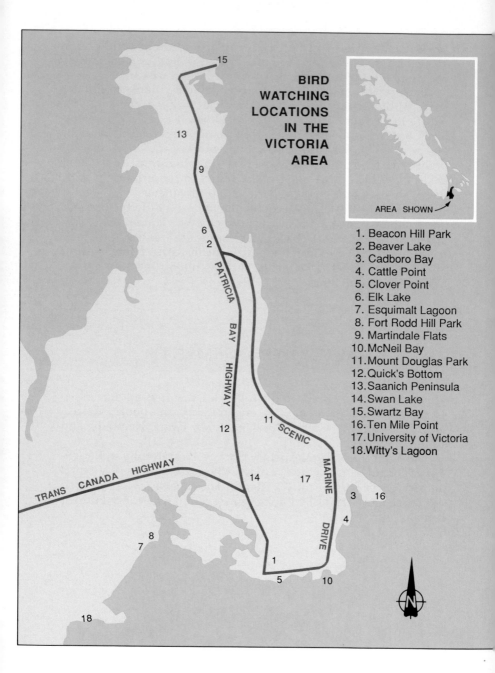

BIRD WATCHING LOCATIONS IN THE VICTORIA AREA

AREA SHOWN

1. Beacon Hill Park
2. Beaver Lake
3. Cadboro Bay
4. Cattle Point
5. Clover Point
6. Elk Lake
7. Esquimalt Lagoon
8. Fort Rodd Hill Park
9. Martindale Flats
10. McNeil Bay
11. Mount Douglas Park
12. Quick's Bottom
13. Saanich Peninsula
14. Swan Lake
15. Swartz Bay
16. Ten Mile Point
17. University of Victoria
18. Witty's Lagoon

BIRDS IN THE CITY

INTRODUCTION

THE URBAN AREAS OF BRITISH COLUMBIA provide some of the most exciting birdwatching opportunities in the province. Many birds have adapted well to these busy environments; in fact their variety and abundance in the city can be overwhelming. Some urban areas retain parts of natural habitats, and the limiting factors that most affect birds are human disturbance and the availability of suitable feeding and nesting sites. Some of the more successful birds, such as House Sparrows, European Starlings, and Rock Doves , have adapted so well to living alongside us that in some situations they are regarded as pests. Nevertheless, these common birds provide living natural history in the urban scene.

For anyone who cares about the environment, birds can provide a very real and tangible way of identifying with nature. Whether on a busy street in Victoria or in a remote part of Goldstream Provincial Park, birds are everywhere around us, easy to see and appreciate without the need for special knowledge or equipment. Over the last decade more and more people have realized this and have taken up birdwatching in their spare time. Today it is the fastest growing recreational activity in the western world. Whether we go out on a hike to look for birds, or merely enjoy them as part of another recreational activity, birdwatching greatly enhances our appreciation of the natural world.

The back yard can be one of the best places to begin watching birds, but it is by no means the only place to find them. Some of the manicured or wild parks in and around Victoria are ideal areas to see a great variety of species that do not normally occur in the heart of the city. These include warblers, flycatchers, hawks, ducks, owls and others.

Parks like Beacon Hill can provide some intriguing and enjoyable opportunities for observing how birds have adapted to city life. The Great Blue Herons that nest there have learned to tolerate us. Other birds like ducks, pigeons, House Sparrows, and geese have adapted so well to inner city life that they have extended their breeding seasons well into the colder months by taking advantage of food and nesting sites provided by humans. A warm ledge or roof on an office building provides some birds, like Glaucous-winged Gulls and Killdeers, with a protected and safe nesting site. Other birds also make use of man-made nesting locations; swallows and wrens for example, will use a variety of odd sites — under the eaves of a house, or a convenient hole in a street lamp.

It is quite possible to create suitable "natural" habitats for birds in the garden, although you are more likely to attract Bewick's Wrens and chickadees and House Finches, rather than anything more exotic.

To appreciate fully the diversity of bird life in the city, it is best to venture out into some of the undisturbed areas that have been conserved in the midst of the urban environment. The birds to be found around Victoria are those that are looking for habitats similar to the natural areas outside the city; selecting the habitat for the type of birds you hope to watch will greatly improve the chances of a rewarding birdwatching sortie.

Coastal areas of Greater Victoria provide a diversity of natural habitats — dry, open forest, coastal rain forest, rocky and sandy shore, estuary, freshwater, saltwater, and tidal lagoons, all within a few miles of the city centre. There are also many urban equivalents of these habitats. A well-wooded neighbourhood will attract many of the forest birds; a breakwater is likely to attract birds of the rocky shore, and at the same time, offer a vantage point for viewing sea birds.

The best tactic to employ on a birdwatching outing is to decide on a series of habitats to visit, and to go to areas where you know these habitats exist. Not surprisingly, the areas where there are mixtures of habitats will increase your likelihood of seeing more species of birds. Wet areas and open water, surrounded by native trees and agricultural fields, will provide some of the richest urban birdwatching experiences.

HABITATS

Within the city, there are many semi-natural areas that are remnants of the unspoiled landscape that existed before this part of British Columbia experienced increasing exploitation by humans, beginning about 150 years ago. The more formal parks within the city are by no means natural to this part of Canada, but they do provide birds and humans alike with a green oasis within the city which they can use in the absence of pristine areas. The best spots for the birdwatcher to explore are those that closely resemble the native landscape of the province.

Open Dry Coastal Forest

A particularly dry zone exists in the immediate vicinity of Victoria, as any gardener will tell you. The area is known as the Gulf Island Zone, and it is found nowhere else in Canada. Most of the west coast has very high rainfall, caused by the warm, wet Pacific airmass being lifted over the coastal mountains, which cools the moist air and releases it in the form of rain and occasionally snow. Lying east of the mountains of central Vancouver Island, in a strip from the southern tip of the island to Comox, there is an area of "rain shadow," low-lying land which escapes the high rainfall immediately to the west. Here the vegetation is very different, and includes the unique Garry oak and arbutus forests. Much of the original dry coastal forest is gone now, as this land is prized for development; however, patches of it remain along the coast. Even in the city parks, such as Beacon Hill, it is possible to see the remnants of the open dry coast forest: there are still Garry oaks and arbutus, and they do well in the drier situations. In more exposed sites, these tend to be small gnarled trees, but in sheltered spots and gardens they grow large and stately.

The open nature of the dry forest means that many other flowering shrubs and plants can grow beneath and among the trees. In April and May, ground flora becomes particularly attractive. Watch at this time of year for Rufous Hummingbirds, which time their arrival to coincide with the early flowering period. These open forests are good areas for woodpeckers such as the Northern Flicker, and for Brown Creepers and Band-tailed Pigeons. Two local specialties, the Bushtit and Hutton's Vireo, can also be found in these drier costal areas.

Coastal Rain Forest

Before Europeans came to this area, coastal rain forest dominated the vegetation. For thousands of years, the trees had grown naturally. It is hard to imagine the spectacular sight that must have met the early visitors to the area, a vista of untouched coastal forest extending over the wetter part of Vancouver Island to the north and west. Although most of this forest has been logged, there are small areas within the city, moreover close by, that have been carefully protected. These give us a good idea of what the forest was like. The woodlands in Elk Lake and Beaver Lake Regional Parks, and those of Mount Douglas, Thomas Francis-Freeman King and Mount Work Regional Parks, are all remnants of a forest that was once part of the wildrness.

The most common trees are the massive Douglas firs, western red cedars and western hemlocks. Beneath them are smaller tree species such as red alder and big leaf maple. Much of the coastal forest has a rich understorey of shrubs and other flowering plants, as well as being an excellent habitat for many different kinds of fern. It is no wonder that this rich and varied vegetation supports an equally rich bird fauna. Bald Eagles and other birds of prey nest in the tall trees, woodpeckers use the abundant wood for nesting cavities and the dense shrub and ground cover is wonderful habitat for many smaller birds, especially the Winter Wren. This exciting forest is there for everyone living in and around Victoria to enjoy.

The Coast

Living near the sea means that we have at our doorstep a variety of different habitats that most Canadians go without. Coastal habitats are quite distinct. Broadly speaking, there is sandy shore, rocky shore and river estuary, and of course, adjacent to Victoria, the ocean itself. Here, it is possible to see some of the true ocean species from the vantage points of a boat or the higher cliffs and bluffs. The trip to the mainland takes us through deep water and this too is a good birdwatching area.

There is not a great deal of sandy shore around Victoria and what we have is, for the most part, confined to bays. Here many species of shorebirds will be found in the spring and autumn migration. Consider going early in the day, before most people get there, and you may well be rewarded with some good birdwatching. Even in the middle of the day, it is worth looking to see if there are any cormorants or other seabirds close to shore.

The rocky shores and man-made structures, such as the breakwater at Ogden Point, are attractive to a different group of birds. This is a more hostile environment, being constantly subjected to wave action. Some specialized birds, like the Black Oystercatcher, Rock Sandpiper and Surfbird spend all of their time here, even though to us feeding appears to be difficult. Prey is often hidden or solidly attached for protection from the effects of the waves. Birds have had to evolve feeding strategies to be able to exploit these food sources. To be able to nest on this sort of shore also requires a degree of specialization. The oystercatcher uses a minimal nest: it finds a depression in which to lay its well-camouflaged eggs, just above the high tide line. Rocky shores usually give us a vantage point from which to see out over the deep water: take advantage of this and watch for loons, grebes, diving ducks and seabirds, as well as other birds not normally seen so close to shore, like the Red-necked Phalarope and Black-legged Kittiwake.

The estuary presents yet another coastal habitat important to birds. The estuaries of Colquitz Creek and Goldstream River attract a different group of birds. Like all estuaries, they are rich in nutrients and important areas for waterfowl and shorebirds. They act as refuelling points for migratory birds, which stop off to feed and rest on their journeys. Perhaps the best place to learn about estuarine habitat is at the Freeman King Visitor Centre at Goldstream Provincial Park, which is open daily during the summer. There is also a trail that leads out into the marsh from the centre. The displays and information available from the Nature House at Witty's Lagoon Regional Park also cover many of the birds found in estuaries.

The open water around Victoria is best viewed from a boat or high vantage point, which allows the birdwatcher to see farther out to sea. Such a place to visit is Clover Point where, close to the shore, there is deep water. There are some birds that spend all the year, except the breeding season, on the open water — such as the shearwaters and diving seabirds. These are specialized in their own way to exploit this habitat. They are very strong swimmers and fliers, and are able to ride out the toughest storms. They may dive to considerable depths to catch fish or skim food from the surface of the water.

Wetlands

Any habitat where there is open freshwater or even a damp marshy area is attractive to all sorts of birds. Ducks feed and breed in these habitats, while other birds, such as gulls, come to drink and bathe. The ponds in Beacon Hill Park can produce some notable birds, such as the Eurasian Wigeon. Perhaps the best wetland to visit is Swan Lake, which has a staffed Nature House open throughout the year. Here you are likely to see marsh birds like grebes and rails, gulls, ducks, Mute Swans and American Coots; there are also bird blinds to make watching even easier and more enjoyable.

There are also many other wetland habitats, such as flooded fields and sewage ponds. The vegetation surrounding these areas is likely to contain willows and alders, and a close look here will often reveal a variety of small perching birds.

Another rich wetland habitat in Victoria is the coastal lagoon. Here, freshwater streams and rivers flow into a natural lagoon which in some cases, such as Albert Head Lagoon, has been completely cut off from the sea. These areas are rich in a variety of waterbirds. There is a string of these lagoons west of Victoria off the road to Sooke.

To the northwest of Victoria is Goldstream Provincial Park, which has another wetland type — a fast flowing river. This is a good place to visit to see the American Dipper, which forages underwater and along the banks. A variety of forest birds may be found in the moister canyon areas of the river. The river has a spectacular run of salmon in the fall; chinook, chum and coho salmon all spawn in the lower reaches and are well worth going to see. The salmon attract hundreds of gulls and mergansers, which feed on the dead and dying fish and their eggs.

BEACON HILL PARK

Over 120 different kinds of birds have been seen over the years by birdwatchers strolling through this popular city park. Highlights include nesting Great Blue Herons, Bald Eagles and Common Ravens in the tall fir trees. The rare Eurasian Wigeon, and many other west coast specialties, readily accept hand-outs from park visitors.

DOWNTOWN VICTORIA

The open parkland-type habitat, with its manicured gardens in the heart of Victoria, attracts many songbirds, predators and gulls. Peregrine Falcons occasionally perch on city buildings, Cooper's Hawks dart between trees bordering streets, and seabirds are constantly flying over the city between roosting and feeding sites.

PONDS/SLOUGHS

Permanent ponds are used by a wide variety of birds for feeding, resting, bathing and breeding. Swallows and flycatchers snap up insects in the air; herons, blackbirds and sparrows patrol the shores; and many songbirds nest in the protective cover of shrubs and grasses.

MARINE COAST

Victoria's rocky shorelines, offshore islands and open ocean habitats are home for an amazing variety of marine birds. Cliffs and rocky headlands provide good vantage points to view west coast specialties like Peregrine Falcon, Black Oystercatcher, Black Turnstone, Rhinoceros Auklet, Marbled Murrelet and Tufted Puffin.

WETLANDS

Brackish lagoons, lakes, rivers and marshy habitats provide exciting birdwatching opportunities. During migration periods over 50 species of shorebirds, ducks, loons, grebes and other waterbirds can be tallied in a single day here.

GARDENS

Known across Canada as "The Garden City," Victoria has
thousands of private and commercial flower gardens which are
maintained throughout the year. Many are associated with
private residences and commercial tourist attractions, but some
of the largest are available to birdwatchers. Be
sure to visit the gardens and forests at the
University of Victoria or public parks.

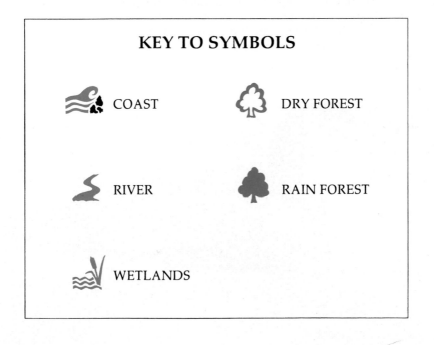

BIRDS OF VICTORIA

KEY TO SYMBOLS

COAST

DRY FOREST

RIVER

RAIN FOREST

WETLANDS

COMMON LOON

Gavia immer

larger than seagull-sized

THE BIRD ON OUR DOLLAR COIN is the Common Loon, a bird that epitomizes Canada's wilderness. It has two distinct plumages. In summer the large black bill, black velvety head with a white necklace, and black back with small checkered white spots, are distinctive. In winter the bird is generally a uniform brown-black above, and white below. It may be distinguished from the smaller Pacific Loon by its wider bill. The top and back of the head of the Pacific Loon is a solid silvery-gray.

The Common Loon is present around Victoria throughout the year, but it is most common from mid-October to mid-May. Sometimes loose flocks, up to fifty or so birds, may be seen in spring and autumn migration periods, but most sightings are of single birds. It frequents sheltered bays, coves, and lagoons along sea coasts. A few can be found on our freshwater lakes, especially Elk, Thetis and Beaver Lakes, but there are no recent breeding records for this area.

Loons dive for fish, often swimming to depths of 55-60 m, propelled by their powerful webbed feet. Most dives last less than thirty seconds but can last up to three minutes. The Common Loon feeds mainly on sculpins, Pacific herring, and other small near-shore fishes. Watch for them anywhere along Victoria's shoreline. Clover Point, the Ogden Point breakwater and off Esquimalt Lagoon are particularily good vantage points.

PIED-BILLED GREBE

Podilymbus podiceps

smaller than crow-sized

THE PIED-BILLED GREBE is a small, dumpy, brown waterbird with a short neck and a short, stout bill. During the breeding season, it has a black throat patch and a black ring around a whitish bill, from which it gets its name.

Pied-billed Grebes are present throughout the year but are much more numerous from September to April when migrating birds from the interior of British Columbia make their way to the coast. They are found on saltwater, but unlike other wintering grebes, they are also commonly found on freshwater lakes, such as Elk and Thetis lakes. They can often be shy, keeping close to vegetation around the edges of the water; this is where to look for them. The Victoria area has the second highest number of Pied-billed Grebes reported in British Columbia during Christmas Bird Counts. The birds are often seen with American Coots, and some puddle ducks. When disturbed they sink underwater without a ripple. They feed on a wide variety of prey but mostly small fishes, aquatic insects and snails.

HORNED GREBE
Podiceps auritus
smaller than crow-sized

THE COLOURS OF THIS SMALL GREBE are entirely different between seasons, except for the red eye. In summer it is a striking bird with a rufous neck, black head with yellow ear tufts and dark back with rusty brown sides. In winter it is drab, generally dark grey-brown above and white below, including the cheek, throat and breast.

It is chiefly a saltwater bird of sheltered areas where it can be found regularly from October to April. Numbers tallied during Christmas Bird Counts in Victoria are the highest reported in Canada.

In winter the Horned Grebe feeds entirely on fishes and marine invertebrates such as snails, small clams and crustaceans. It dives to a depth of nine metres and averages about 25 seconds underwater. Occasionally groups of five or more will feed as a team, diving together to surround a school of small Pacific herring or sandlance.

DOUBLE-CRESTED CORMORANT
Phalacrocorax auritus
larger than seagull-sized

BRANDT'S CORMORANT
Phalacrocorax penicillatus
larger than seagull-sized

PELAGIC CORMORANT
Phalacrocorax pelagicus
seagull-sized

OFTEN CALLED "EITHER-ENDERS," cormorants are amongst the most common and easily identified of all seabird groups around the Victoria waterfront. The three species can be told apart in flight with a little practice. The Pelagic Cormorant, the smallest of the three, is slender in flight and has a very straight neck, a small head, and a rapid wing beat. Brandt's is stockier, with a large head and a straight neck, while the Double-crested Cormorant is stocky, with a thick neck and large head. It flies with a heavy wing beat and often with a distinct kink in the neck. Up close, look for the differently coloured throat patches: yellow to orange in Double-crested, red in Pelagic, and blue in Brandt's, but with buff-coloured throat feathers. In late spring and summer Brandt's also shows long white feathers on the neck and back, the Double-crested develops two white ear tufts, while the

Top: Double-crested Cormorant
Left: Pelagic Cormorant
Right: Brandt's Cormorant

Pelagic cormorant sports two white flank patches.

The Double-crested Cormorant is the only species to visit freshwater lakes, such as Elk, Swan and Blankinsop, and can often be seen flying in formation over the busiest parts of Victoria.

All three species breed in the Victoria area, on offshore islands. The Double-crested Cormorant is the most numerous. Nearly three-quarters of the British Columbia population breeds on Mandarte and Chain Islands near Victoria. They build their large, bulky stick nests on rocky slopes. In 1987 three Brandt's Cormorants were found on Race Rocks just west of Victoria. The Pelagic Cormorant, a widespread breeder, prefers cliff ledges on offshore islands and tall, steep rocky headlands on which to build its seaweed nest.

Although all three species can be found throughout the year in Victoria, winter is the best time to find them. In fact, more cormorants are counted during Christmas Bird Counts in Victoria than anywhere else in Canada. The Double-crested Cormorant is best seen at Elk Lake, Portage Inlet, the Gorge, and Esquimault Lagoon. The Brandt's Cormorant is often seen from the ferries passing through Active Pass, about mid-point in the trip between Vancouver Island and the mainland, and off Ten Mile point in Victoria where flocks pass by during daily feeding forays. It is most common from September to April.

Unlike other waterbirds, the webbed feet of cormorants are unusual in that the web connects four toes instead of three. This allows the birds to cling to rocky cliffs as well as pursue shoaling fish such as Pacific herring and sandlance, or locate solitary fish hiding among seaweeds or under rocks.

GREAT BLUE HERON
Ardea herodias
larger than seagull-sized

HERE IN VICTORIA, Great Blue Herons are present throughout the year. They are distinctive in flight, as they trail their long legs behind them and carry their necks bent in an S-shape. The birds are large, about 1.2 m tall, with a wingspan of 2.1 m, and generally have a blue-grey body.

Herons can be found wherever there is shallow water — salt, fresh, or brackish. In winter, large numbers are found at Sidney and Esquimalt Lagoon, while in summer birdwatchers are attracted to their nesting colony in Beacon Hill Park. Here the noise and odour of white-washed lawns below nesting fir trees will be remembered!

The Great Blue Heron is a patient hunter, whether standing in water waiting for fish to appear, or in a dry field waiting for a mouse to come within striking distance. They catch their prey, which also includes frogs, snakes, crabs and insects, with a lightning thrust of the beak. At times, when the prey seems longer than the heron is capable of eating, swallowing can take some time.

MUTE SWAN

Cygnus olor

larger than seagull-sized

MUTE SWANS, originally from Europe and Asia, were first introduced into Victoria about 1889. They are now a familiar sight on lakes, ponds, inlets, and estuaries around the city, where feral populations exist. Largest numbers, however, are found in the vicinity of Cowichan Bay, north of Victoria.

This large white swan often arches its wings over its back, particularly when displaying or behaving aggressively. The pinkish or orange bill with a black knob at its base is characteristic. Two other species of swans likely to be seen near the city as they migrate to and from their breeding grounds are the Tundra Swan and the Trumpeter Swan. The former usually has a small yellow spot on the black bill, the latter a solid black bill. In addition, the Mute Swan is less vocal than the others, usually making only a hissing sound. It is the only one likely to be seen within Victoria itself.

Mute Swans build a very large nest of grasses, reeds, and cattails, usually in shallow water. Up to eight eggs may be laid in early April but most egg-laying occurs in late May and early June. It takes up to 150 days before the young can fly. It is not wise to venture near a nesting swan as there are many instances of people being attacked and hurt.

CANADA GOOSE
Branta canadensis
larger than seagull-sized

THE CANADA GOOSE is one of the most widely recognized birds in Canada. There are many different subspecies which, with practise, can be separated by size, colour, and voice. Four of these have been seen in the Victoria area, mostly in the spring and autumn when they are on migration. Most common is the western race, which is a darker brown and lacks the noticeably pale breast of the others.

Canada Geese can be found here at any time of the year, as many have become semi-tame and will vie with Mallards, Glaucous-winged Gulls, and American Coots for scraps of bread and bird seed. It is also possible to see truly wild geese, especially during migration. Witty's Lagoon and the farm fields of the Saanich peninsula are good places to watch for them.

The Canada Goose builds its grass nest on the ground, usually near water. The female lines the nest with down from her breast and uses the down to cover the eggs, keeping them warm and drawing less attention to them when the adults leave the nest. Up to fourteen eggs may be laid, usually in late April, but occasionally as early as mid-March. Incubation takes 28 days, and another 63 days are required for full flight. Apparently many geese mate for life and sometimes family groups can be distinguished by careful observation during migration.

MALLARD
Anas platyrhynchos
seagull-sized

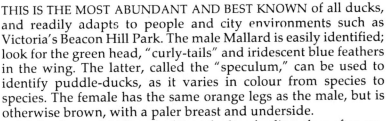

THIS IS THE MOST ABUNDANT AND BEST KNOWN of all ducks, and readily adapts to people and city environments such as Victoria's Beacon Hill Park. The male Mallard is easily identified; look for the green head, "curly-tails" and iridescent blue feathers in the wing. The latter, called the "speculum," can be used to identify puddle-ducks, as it varies in colour from species to species. The female has the same orange legs as the male, but is otherwise brown, with a paler breast and underside.

Mallards are dabbling ducks, and when feeding, they often up-end to reach below the surface for waterweeds and other vegetation, seeds, grain, small insects and snails. Some Mallards are present year-round in Victoria, but birds from the north and the interior also winter here — well over five thousand birds in the city environment.

The Mallard has a long breeding season on the south coast of British Columbia. Downy young can be found as early as March and as late as mid-November. Despite the fact that the female may already be paired, it is a common sight in the spring, especially in city parks, to see a hen pursued by three or more drakes.

NORTHERN PINTAIL
Anas acuta
seagull-sized

OF ALL DUCKS, the Northern Pintail is the most graceful and elegant. The male's plumage is striking, with its chestnut brown head, white neck and gray body, and long, thin black central tailfeathers. The female is a subtle mixture of browns. Both are easily recognized in flight from a distance by their long necks and pointed "pin" tails.

The species is most abundant during migration, especially in autumn when both young and adults pass by Victoria in large flocks from August to late October. Each year some will stop and winter around Victoria, where they can be found in marshes, wet fields, estuaries, and lagoons within the city. The Northern Pintail does not breed here.

The scientific name for this slender bird is derived from Latin words which mean "duck with a pointed tail." The Northern Pintail eats a variety of plants and animals but, while here, eats mostly farm crops and marsh vegetation.

NORTHERN SHOVELER

Anas clypeata

larger than crow-sized

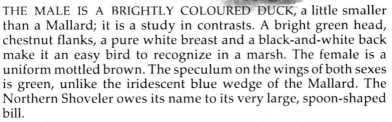

THE MALE IS A BRIGHTLY COLOURED DUCK, a little smaller than a Mallard; it is a study in contrasts. A bright green head, chestnut flanks, a pure white breast and a black-and-white back make it an easy bird to recognize in a marsh. The female is a uniform mottled brown. The speculum on the wings of both sexes is green, unlike the iridescent blue wedge of the Mallard. The Northern Shoveler owes its name to its very large, spoon-shaped bill.

The Northern Shoveler is present throughout the year around Victoria, occasionally breeding here, but is most common in the non-breeding season, from mid-October to the end of March. It can be found on any suitable shallow pond or lake, or with other waterfowl in flooded fields. Good viewing spots include Quick's Bottom, Swan Lake, Esquimalt Lagoon, and the flooded fields of the Saanich peninsula.

Shovelers are dabbling ducks, and feed in shallow water by sifting the surface water for both plant food, such as seeds of water plants, and for small aquatic animals. Its bill is wonderfully adapted for this; as well as being large, it has a sieve-like inside edge which enables the bird to screen its food from muddy water.

AMERICAN WIGEON

Anas americana

larger than crow-sized

THE MALE AMERICAN WIGEON is readily identified by the white on its forehead and crown, which gave the duck its old and not very flattering name of Baldpate. The female, as is often the case with ducks, is brown, an adaptation to avoid detection by predators during incubation. Both male and female have a striking white breast and large white wing patches, which are most visible when the birds are in flight.

The American Wigeon is a very common winter resident in Victoria and on the south coast of British Columbia. It is present in numbers from October through March. In some years this duck is the most numerous bird seen on Christmas Bird Counts. Infrequently one or two pairs may breed in the area.

Look for this puddle duck anywhere that large patches of grass are found, such as golf courses and parks. It also frequents sewage outlets, agricultural fields, and marshy habitats. This gregarious bird is predominantly vegetarian, grazing on grasses and sedges as well as on marine algae on the shoreline.

Each winter another rarer, but closely related species, the Eurasian Wigeon *(A. penelope)*, identified by its rusty-brown head, can be spotted among our flocks of American Wigeon.

GREATER SCAUP
Aythya marila
crow-sized

THERE ARE TWO SPECIES of scaup, or blue-bills, found in British Columbia, but the more common on saltwater is the Greater Scaup. Both species look almost identical and are always a problem to tell apart. Look for the more rounded head of the Greater Scaup (the Lesser Scaup's head appears more domed) and in good light, the male Greater Scaup's head shows a green gloss, compared to the blue or purple gloss of the Lesser Scaup. The females are brown and show a white patch at the base of the bill, a mark that is visible from quite a distance. In flight they present a very black and white look, and have a white trailing edge on the upper hind part of the wings. The white wing-stripe of the Greater Scaup extends through most of the wing.

The Greater Scaup is a common sight on the sea and in the bays around Victoria from November through March. It can be seen in most sheltered coastal areas, and Esquimalt Lagoon and Clover Point are good places to look. A few individuals of both species remain in Victoria waters through the summer.

HARLEQUIN DUCK
Histrionicus histrionicus
crow-sized

VICTORIA'S SHORELINE IS THE BEST PLACE to see this brightly patterned duck. Only the male Wood Duck rivals it as the "best dressed waterfowl." The grey-blue body of the male is boldly marked with white stripes and spots on the breast, back of the head, base of the bill and behind the eye. These contrast beautifully with the rich chestnut flanks. The female is generally a subdued grey-brown, with a dusky light belly and with two or three spots on the head.

The Harlequin Duck is fairly common throughout the year anywhere rocky shorelines are found, especially in the vicinity of McNeill Bay, Ten Mile Point, Holland Point, and the many off-shore islands. The species does not breed in Victoria, but in April pairs fly to fresh water streams on Vancouver Island and the interior to breed. As early as May, the males return to Victoria to moult out of their garish nuptial plumage, leaving the females on the fast-flowing streams to incubate the eggs and raise the brood.

Harlequins feed on a variety of marine invertebrates that are common on rocky shallows. Small snails, worms, mussels, clams, crabs and other crustaceans make up their diet.

SURF SCOTER

Melanitta perspicillata

larger than crow-sized

THE SURF SCOTER is an attractive, large sea duck. The male is black, except for a white patch on the back of the neck and the top of the head. It has orangish feet and legs, and its bill is large and brightly marked with black, white and orange. The female is much drabber and is largely brown, with some white behind the bill and below the eye.

Surf Scoters are found on saltwater. Although they are essentially a winter duck in Coastal British Columbia, some non-breeding birds remain in the Victoria area year round. Spring departures, for northern breeding grounds, occur mainly in April. By September, many will have returned to the coastal waters around Victoria.

Watch for Surf Scoters in shallow marine and brackish areas, and in the rough water well offshore — as their name implies. In spring, large rafts may be seen off Clover Point and Royal Road. These groups, of 1500 or more, may be feeding on herring fry recently hatched from nearby kelp beds. Normally, though, they feed on mussels and clams which they wrestle from rocks or prod from sandy sea floors.

WHITE-WINGED SCOTER
Melanitta fusca
larger than crow-sized

LARGEST OF THE DUCKS found in British Columbia, the White-winged Scoter is a sea duck and, except during the breeding season, is found almost exclusively on salt water. The male is essentially black, with a small white mark through the eye and a white patch on each wing. This white can be hidden at times but is very noticeable in flight, and is a good way of distinguishing the species. The female is a fairly uniform dark brown and shows the white wing patch as well.

The White-winged Scoter frequents marine and brackish waters throughout the year and is often found with rafts of Surf Scoters. The peak movement to breeding grounds in spring occurs in April; the return in autumn peaks in September. This bird is often seen in the calmer waters of Cordova Bay, in Satellite Channel, and off Esquimalt Lagoon and Clover Point. Watch for it also at Patricia Bay, by the airport, and during the ferry crossing to the mainland.

During the winter, it feeds by diving for shellfish, snails and crustaceans which are abundant along the coast. It uses its wings to reach prey, and prefers more shallow feeding sites than does the Surf Scoter.

COMMON GOLDENEYE
Bucephala clangula
crow-sized

BARROW'S GOLDENEYE
Bucephala islandica
crow-sized

BOTH SPECIES OF GOLDENEYES are seen around Victoria but only the Common Goldeneye (above) is present throughout the year. Identifying males is easy. The male Barrow's Goldeneye has a comma-shaped white patch on the face, compared to the round white patch in the male Common Goldeneye; the back of the Barrow's is black, spotted with white, and in the Common Goldeneye the back appears much whiter. The Barrow's Goldeneye has a dark line of feathers that separates the white breast from the white flanks, whereas the white in the Common Goldeneye is continuous. The females, however, are difficult to tell apart; look for the Barrow's Goldeneye's steeper forehead and shorter, more orange bill.

Both species frequent a variety of marine and freshwater habitats. The Common Goldeneye is widely distributed along all

41

shorelines whereas the Barrow's Goldeneye frequents only rocky shorelines. The latter, at times, is a difficult species to locate here, but two favorite habitats are the Goldstream estuary and Patricia Bay. Southern coastal areas support the highest number of wintering Barrow's Goldeneyes in the world, and it is estimated that British Columbia has sixty to ninety percent of the world's breeding population.

Barrow's Goldeneye

BUFFLEHEAD
Bucephala albeola
smaller than crow-sized

THIS IS A SMALL DIVING DUCK that is related to the goldeneyes. Buffleheads rarely breed here on the west coast of British Columbia, preferring the interior and prairie provinces. However, large numbers arrive in the fall to spend the winter on the estuaries, coastal rivers and lakes, and even on the sea. During the winter they can be seen on virtually any of the lakes and ponds around Victoria. Swan Lake Nature Centre, Oak Bay and the Esquimalt shoreline are good places to watch for them.

The males are a sharply contrasting pattern of black and white, with iridescent purples and greens refracting from the black portion of the head. The females are dark brown and have white patches on the head. White on the inner edges of the wings is prominent in flight.

The Bufflehead dives for and eats small aquatic animals and insects. It prefers to feed in the shallow and productive intertidal zone. With such an abundant food supply, it is little wonder that Victoria's wintering Bufflehead population is higher than that of any other place in Canada.

HOODED MERGANSER
Lophodytes cucullatus
crow-sized

THIS SMALL, CRESTED DIVER is found only in North America, and Victoria is its major wintering area in Canada. The male is handsome, with a narrow black bill, black body, rusty sides and a spectacular white crest, disk-like and bordered in black. The female is similar in shape but is generally brown with a rusty coloured crest.

It prefers freshwater lakes and ponds where as many as four hundred may be found in winter. Elk and Thetis Lakes and Esquimault Lagoon are favourite habitats. Small flocks also occur in sheltered coastal waters. It is regularly seen from August to April.

Hooded Mergansers occasionally nest near Victoria, usually as a result of nest box programs set up primarily for the less common Wood Duck. Both species take readily to boxes erected near lakes and marshes.

Unlike its larger relatives, the Common and Red-breasted Mergansers, the Hooded Merganser's diet is balanced between fishes and invertebrates, including snails, insects, crayfish and other small crustaceans.

TURKEY VULTURE
Cathartes aura
larger than seagull-sized

SOUTHERN VANCOUVER ISLAND and the adjacent Gulf Islands are the best places in Canada to find the Turkey Vulture. This is a large black, lumbering bird, with a silver-grey lining to its underwings. It appears headless in flight due to its short neck and small bare head.

Turkey Vultures are normally seen in flight; they appear to soar effortlessly, seldom flapping their wings and often rocking from side to side. They hold their wings in a shallow V, which is a useful clue to their identification when viewed from a distance. They are able to soar for extended periods by using thermal air currents, which buoy them up. They often locate their food — usually carrion — by smell, even though it may be hidden under denser vegetation.

The Turkey Vulture may be seen in the Victoria area in all months of the year, but the bulk of the coastal population arrives from the south in late March. Most of them nest and leave again by mid-October. From early September to early October hundreds of vultures gather at favourite staging areas, on the larger offshore islands and near Beachy Head and Sooke, before flying in loose flocks to wintering areas in California and Mexico. It is not uncommon to see up to one hundred or more soaring over the shoreline and rural areas of the city in September. They await the ideal climatic conditions that will allow them to begin a series of soaring and gliding flights across Juan de Fuca Strait and southwards.

OSPREY
Pandion haliaetus
seagull-sized

THIS LARGE, LONG-WINGED BIRD OF PREY can be seen around Victoria from spring through autumn. Its wings are light below and are often held in a W-shape. A brown patch under the wing at the "wrist" is noticeable. Close up, the white head with dark eyestripe is distinctive. Male and female are similar.

Most Ospreys arrive here during the first two weeks of April and by October, most have departed for southern winter areas. They nest near estuaries and larger lakes, such as Thetis, Elk, and Langford Lakes and Witty's Lagoon. Bulky stick nests are built in April, usually atop living trees with dead tops, and are used year after year. The nesting cycle takes about three months, 43 days for incubation and another fifty days for the young to fly.

The Osprey feeds entirely on fish. It catches them by quartering the water and watching. When it sees a fish, it hovers before diving into the water feet-first. This is a skill that is learned, and young birds are at a risk of starving unless they acquire the skills rapidly. Ospreys have sharp spines on their feet and, unlike other birds of prey, have two toes pointing backwards and two pointing forwards. These features help them to hold slippery, struggling fish. When they fly, they hold their catch like a torpedo — the most aerodynamically efficient way possible.

Ospreys are often pursued by Bald Eagles, which frequently sit and wait for them and then try to intimidate them into dropping their catch.

BALD EAGLE
Haliaeetus leucocephalus
larger than seagull-sized

MORE BALD EAGLES ARE SEEN in the Victoria area than any other bird of prey. The adult is distinctive with its all white head and tail. The young bird, however, is more difficult to identify and may be confused with the Golden Eagle. Both have dark brown bodies, but the immature Bald Eagle lacks the broad white band at the base of the tail typical of immature Golden Eagles. It takes five years before Bald Eagles obtain full adult plumage.

Bald Eagles are most common near water and will often spend hours sitting on a snag overlooking a lake, estuary or the sea. The largest numbers are reported by ferry passengers travelling through Active Pass. In winter as many as one hundred or more may be seen soaring, or perched on trees in the Pass. They are adept at catching fish, which they pluck from just below the surface with their talons. They also feed on carrion found along the shore or floating in the water. The Bald Eagle frequently steals food from Ospreys by diving at them and chasing them until they drop their fish.

Bald Eagles build huge stick nests in trees and will often re-use a nest year after year, the nest eventually reaching an immense size. The largest nest measured was 3.6 m in diameter and 3 m in height. Eggs may be laid from mid-February through late June and it is rare to find young still in the nest after mid-August.

COOPER'S HAWK

Accipiter cooperii

crow-sized

THERE ARE FEW PLACES IN BRITISH COLUMBIA where Cooper's Hawk can be seen more regularly than in Victoria. In fact, the highest winter numbers in Canada, tallied during Christmas Bird Counts, have been recorded here. This is a forest hawk with short, rounded wings and a long tail that is used as a rudder when pursuing woodland birds. Adults are similar and have dark blue-grey upperparts, reddish bars on the underside and a banded tail. The tail is rounded at the tip, not square as in its smaller relative, the Sharp-shinned Hawk (*A. striatus*).

This medium sized raptor is most often spotted soaring over mixed woodlands where it nests. Stick nests are built in trees, from 5 m to 25 m above the ground. City parks are favourite breeding locations; one nest was a mere 2.4 m directly over a well travelled park path. Three or four eggs are laid from late April to late May. Incubation lasts about thirty-five days; about thirty-two days after hatching the young can fly.

The Cooper's Hawk has declined in numbers in most parts of its North American range, except here in the West. Watch for it as it makes lightning fast raids on the birds at your feeding station.

MERLIN
Falco columbarius
larger than robin-sized

FORMERLY KNOWN AS THE PIGEON HAWK, the Merlin is a jay-sized falcon with long pointed wings. The birds around Victoria belong to a race that breeds along the west coast of British Columbia and are darker than those found in the rest of Canada. The only other small falcon is the American Kestrel; the two can be told apart as the Merlin is generally darker above and below, and lacks the "double moustache" of the kestrel.

The Merlin is resident on southern Vancouver Island but is most common from September through March. During the breeding season, it inhabits woodland areas. Its eggs are laid in old Steller's Jay or Northwestern Crow nests. One pair even used an old Pileated Woodpecker nest cavity. The Merlin feeds on small birds which it catches in a spectacular aerial chase, usually out in the open or above the trees. Outside the breeding season, it is most often seen in open areas, such as fields adjoining woodland and along the shore. It will also hunt through back yards, especially near feeders. If you are lucky enough to be on a regular hunting route, you may catch a fleeting glimpse of a Merlin passing at high speed.

PEREGRINE FALCON
Falco peregrinus
crow-sized

BIRDWATCHERS IN VICTORIA have a good chance of seeing a Peregrine Falcon, especially from September through February. In flight, look for a bird with narrow, pointed wings and a shallow but rapid wing beat. When perched, notice the moustache stripe and the slate-grey backs of the adults and brown backs of the immature falcons. Underparts are barred in adults and streaked in immatures.

The Peregrine Falcon feeds on small shorebirds and pigeons, and larger perching birds like starlings. It catches prey by direct pursuit from a power dive. This method involves the Peregrine's circling under a flock of birds to force them to a great height, whereupon he will casually break away. As the flock returns downward, the Peregrine will "stoop" with great speed, singling out a victim before it can reach the safety of the trees. Look for Peregrines wherever large numbers of prey gather — along the seashore or over fields.

Between 100 and 110 pairs of Peregrine Falcons breed in British Columbia, mostly on the Queen Charlotte Islands. However, a few pairs breed in the Gulf Islands. Fortunately, in British Columbia there is no evidence to suggest that DDT has affected the reproductive success of this once-threatened species.

RING-NECKED PHEASANT
Phasianus colchicus
larger than seagull-sized

ORIGINALLY AN ASIAN BIRD, the Ring-necked Pheasant was introduced to British Columbia at Victoria in 1882 as a sporting bird from England, where it was reared for the aristocracy to shoot. The first few birds to arrive died, but the next year 25 pheasants from China were successfully introduced. The population increased greatly, partly through the expansion of wild populations and partly through provincial government breeding programs. Today, however, numbers are declining as its farmland habitat disappears. The spectacular plumage of the male is a familiar sight in the fields around the edge of the city, and it may even be seen in our wooded parks and marshes.

During the spring breeding season, the males collect a harem of up to five hens, which they then attempt to protect from the advances of male rivals. The females are much less gaudily coloured than their mates. They incubate the eggs, which have been laid in a grass-lined depression on the ground — often hidden below a bush. The size of a normal clutch varies, but usually consists of 9 to 13 olive-brown eggs. Sometimes more than one female will lay in the same nest and eggs will literally overflow the edges. Twenty-eight eggs are the most that have been found in one nest in Victoria. When this happens, very few actually hatch.

CALIFORNIA QUAIL
Callipepla californica
robin-sized

VICTORIA LEADS THE PROVINCE in population of this attractive bird, first introduced to British Columbia in Victoria in the early 1860s. Its numbers increased gradually, occasionally reflecting the susceptibility of this southern species to severe winters, and peaked in the 1950s. Since then it has slowly decreased as the city grows, and suburbs consume its favourite haunts. It can still be found in a variety of habitats, including open shrublands, large gardens, golf courses, and powerline clearings.

These plump birds, smaller than a city pigeon, generally have blue-grey upperparts with brown wings. The belly feathers are scale-like in appearance. Both sexes have a "top knot" or curved, black plume of feathers on the head, more noticeable in the males. Males also have a black head with bold white stripes.

Nests are built on the ground in dense vegetation, and consist mainly of grasses, leaves and rootlets. The nesting cycle, from egg to fledgling, lasts about a month, and larger coveys of two or more families may be encountered in the autumn and winter.

A distant relative, the Mountain Quail *(Oreortys pictus)*, may still be present in the hills surrounding Victoria, although only a few confirmed sightings have been recorded in the past decade.

AMERICAN COOT

Fulica americana

smaller than crow-sized

THIS CHICKEN-LIKE BIRD, most frequently found on lakes, marshes and sloughs around the city, is readily identified by its behaviour and markings. It bobs its head as it walks and swims, making it look like a comical clockwork toy. Its generally blackish plumage is highlighted by a white bill and white patch under its short tail. Its toes are lobed and flattened to help with swimming and walking on mud, from which it derives its popular western name, "mudhen."

It is most common here in winter. Autumn migrants begin arriving in October and numbers increase through the winter, especially on Elk and Thetis Lakes, Esquimalt Lagoon, and Swan Lake. By early March only a few breeding pairs remain. American Coots feed by diving and tipping for water weeds, small shellfish and shrimps. They also search the edges of ponds and sloughs for insects and snails. They build a floating nest of reeds and rushes amongst the vegetation at the edge of the water by early June, and lay 8 to 12 spotted, buff-coloured eggs.

KILLDEER
Charadrius vociferus
robin-sized

THE KILLDEER is the most widespread of all the shorebirds within the immediate area of the city. A relatively large plover (27 cm long), it is readily identified by its double black breast bands and by its call, *kildee kildee*, after which it is named. Its Latin name, *vociferus*, is no misnomer; it can be heard throughout the year and spends a great deal of time calling.

The Killdeer does not build a nest as such, but digs out a small scrape in the ground which it decorates with small stones, wood chips and pieces of plants. Typically it lays four buff-coloured eggs, well camouflaged with black spots, and may nest twice each summer. The Killdeer has refined the art of decoying predators away from the nest. It will trail a wing and drag a leg under the nose of a would-be predator, only to fly or run off at high speed once it has led the predator away from the nest site. It will even settle onto an imaginary nest, to try and lure the predator away. The Killdeer breeds on old industrial sites and gravel rooftops, as well as on unpaved roads, near golf courses and in any relatively open areas. It is resident on southern Vancouver Island, but numbers are greatest during spring and fall migration.

BLACK OYSTERCATCHER

Haematopus bachmani

crow-sized

THE BLACK OYSTERCATCHER cannot be confused with any other bird. It is a crow-sized, dull black wading bird, with a long, relatively heavy red bill. Long pink legs and feet, and a red eye-ring visible at close range, are also distinctive features.

A visit to Victoria's outer shoreline will almost certainly be rewarded with a view of this attractive bird. It breeds above the tide line and hardly bothers to build a nest at all, but rather decorates a shallow depression — even on bare rock — with pieces of shell and stones. Two or three well camouflaged, spotted eggs are laid. The adults are vociferous at the best of times, but if you happen to wander near a nest they become very noisy indeed.

The Black Oystercatcher feeds mainly on limpets and chitons which it knocks off rocks at tide's edge. It also probes mussel beds for other marine invertebrates and uses its laterally compressed bill (slimmer side to side than top to bottom) to open bivalves such as mussels, clams and oysters.

GREATER YELLOWLEGS

Tringa melanoleuca

smaller than crow-sized

THIS LARGE SANDPIPER sports its characteristic long, yellow legs in both breeding and winter plumage. It can be confused only with its smaller relative, the Lesser Yellowlegs *(T. flavipes)*, whose bill is thin and about equal to the head in length. The longer bill of the Greater Yellowlegs has a slight upward curve. Both species show white rumps when flying and both lack wing stripes. The Greater Yellowlegs usually occurs singly or in small flocks while the Lesser Yellowlegs is far more gregarious — flocks can number in the hundreds.

In Victoria the Greater Yellowlegs has been found in every month of the year but is most numerous during spring migration (mid-April to early May) and during autumn migration (early July to late August). Winter numbers in Victoria are the highest found in Canada. While migrating, both Yellowleg species may be seen feeding and resting in the shallows of lakes, ponds, wet fields and tidal mud flats. Like most shorebirds, they can be approached quite closely, providing a good opportunity for one to appreciate the subtle details of form and behaviour.

BLACK TURNSTONE

Arenaria melanocephala

smaller than robin-sized

STRIKING IS THE BEST TERM to describe this stocky shorebird. In breeding plumage it is generally all black except for a snow-white belly. The non-breeding and winter plumage is a more subdued brown-black in colour. In flight the wings and body flash an intricate and contrasting black-and-white pattern, undoubtedly making it easier for stragglers to stay with the flock. The bird's rattling call, especially when flying, also helps to keep the flock together and certainly lets you know it is near.

The Black Turnstone is the most abundant shorebird of Victoria's rocky shores and pebble beaches, and some may be found regularly at Witty's and Esquimalt lagoons. Occasionally they will feed on the lawns at Clover Point and the Victoria Golf Club.

They are most common in Victoria from late August through March. Once the birds arrive in the autumn they are faithful to favoured wintering locations and do not wander far before they leave again in the spring.

GULLS

COASTAL BRITISH COLUMBIA is one of the best places in Canada to see gulls. In Victoria alone, seventeen different kinds may be seen. Some of these are very rare visitors, others are numerous during migration periods and one is an abundant year-round resident. All can be found near salt water, but a few travel inland to larger lakes, cultivated fields, and landfills. A good place to observe gulls is from the ferry on its trip between the mainland and Vancouver Island. The following six gulls can all be found regularly in season around the city.

BONAPARTE'S GULL

Larus philadelphia
smaller than crow-sized

LOOK FOR THIS SMALL GULL throughout the year but mostly during migration periods. Up to 8,000 can be seen together off the Victoria waterfront and in Active Pass from early to mid-May and from early September through December. In breeding plumage the entire head, including the bill, is black. Outside the breeding season the head is white with a dark spot behind the eye. Immatures are mottled with brown on the back and sides of the body and all have a narrow black tail band. They are noisy when feeding together on small schooling fishes and pelagic crustaceans concentrated by tidal upwellings.

HEERMANN'S GULL

Larus heermanni
larger than crow-sized

THIS MEXICAN VISITOR arrives on southern Vancouver Island after its breeding season, practising a form of reverse migration. The first birds appear in early May and June, but the main influx starts about mid-July and peaks in mid-October, after which the birds move south again. Adults are unmistakable, with contrasting light and dark grey tones to their plumage and a prominent red bill. Immatures are dark brown with a pinkish bill. The Heermann's Gull may be found along rocky shores and islets and often roosts on floating kelp beds. Victoria is the most reliable spot in Canada to see this handsome bird.

Top: Bonaparte's Gull
Bottom: Heermann's Gull

59

MEW GULL
Larus canus
crow-sized

THIS SMALL GULL is more abundant in some winters than is the resident Glaucous-winged Gull. Victoria holds the record for the highest numbers tallied in Canada during Christmas Bird Counts. Adults have a small but solid yellow bill, grey mantle, black wing tips with white patches, and pinkish-yellow legs. The size of body and bill relative to other gulls is the best clue for identifying the greyish-brown young. A few Mew Gulls may be present throughout the year but this species is most common from August through March. It breeds west and north of Victoria. It is seldom found very far offshore and prefers to look for its food in sheltered bays, inlets, lagoons and along tide lines.

CALIFORNIA GULL
Larus californicus
larger than crow-sized

THIS MEDIUM-SIZED VISITOR, in adult plumage, has a yellow bill with a red and black spot, a light grey back, black wing tips and yellow-green legs. Immatures, as with most species of gulls, are difficult to identify, so field guides should be consulted as an aid.

Small numbers appear along the Victoria waterfront in March and April, but the main influx occurs in autumn, from early July through mid-September. Banding returns have shown that Victoria's visiting California Gulls originate from Saskatchewan, Alberta, North Dakota, Montana, Wyoming, Idaho and the coastal states south of British Columbia. Clover Point is a good place to see this bird.

THAYER'S GULL
Larus thayeri
smaller than seagull-sized

ADULT THAYER'S GULLS are similar in many respects to the more familiar Herring Gull, but are smaller (medium-sized), with no black showing on the underwing tips and usually with brown instead of yellow eyes. Nesting in the high Arctic, this species visits Victoria only outside the breeding season. Wintering birds

Top: Mew Gull
Middle: California Gull
Bottom: Thayer's Gull

begin arriving in late September, increasing their numbers through December; by mid-February most have left again for the north. Its immature plumages challenge even the experts. Like some other gulls it also frequents garbage dumps but can be found most often along the shoreline. From October to January Clover Point is the best place in British Columbia to see this gull.

GLAUCOUS-WINGED GULL
Larus glaucescens
seagull-sized

THE GLAUCOUS-WINGED GULL is the most common resident gull of coastal British Columbia and it is this species you will see most often. It is large, with a heavy yellow bill and a red-orange spot on the lower mandible. The adults have a pure white head, except in winter when it is streaked with brown. In flight the wing tips are grey, not black, as in many other gulls. A close relative, the Western Gull, has a darker back, blacker wing tips, and darker underlining on the wings.

Over 28,000 pairs breed in British Columbia, with some of the largest colonies found on Mandarte and Chain Islands near Victoria. In May, the Glaucous-winged Gull builds its nest on the ground using seaweed, grass and other vegetation. It usually lays three olive-brown eggs, which are mottled with darker brown; young hatch in early July. This gull, like many others, has adapted well to humans and can be found in large numbers wherever we inadvertently provide food: garbage dumps (one of the best places to watch gulls), around fishing boats, or at sewage outfalls. It will also scrounge food from people on the beach, at picnic grounds and even from windows of office buildings, on top of which a few pairs will nest.

ROCK DOVE
Columba livia
smaller than crow-sized

MOST PEOPLE CALL THEM PIGEONS. Originally from the Mediterranean regions, they have since been introduced into other parts of the world. Their year-round breeding habits led them to be used as a domesticated source of meat. The species has adapted well to inner city living and the ledges of older buildings provide a good substitute for its more natural habitat of rocky cliffs, from which it gets its name. They also forage in city parks, along seashores, and in cultivated fields.

The birds make a scant nest on a ledge and breed in all months of the year, sometimes raising several broods in a year. The young are fed on "pigeon milk" — a liquid produced in the crop of the adult from predigested food. Pigeons have become pests in most large cities; their excrement builds up on the ledges of the buildings and their sheer numbers are a nuisance. One of the principal predators of the Rock Dove is the Peregrine Falcon, a bird which can be seen on Victoria's buildings from time to time. Cooper's Hawks also prey on this dove.

BAND-TAILED PIGEON
Columba fasciata
smaller than crow-sized

THIS IS TRULY THE WILD PIGEON of British Columbia. Once confined to the southwest coast it is slowly expanding its range eastward and northward in the province. One of the best places to see this bird is still in the environs of Victoria. It is present throughout the year but is most common from May through September. Look for them among the Garry oak trees on golf courses, in city parks, and over the coniferous forests surrounding the city. In autumn and winter they search out berry-producing trees and shrubs and the acorns of the oaks.

Band-tailed Pigeons can be distinguished from the city-dwelling Rock Doves by their bright yellow bills and feet, a white crescent on the back of the neck and a wide grey band on the tip of the tail. Band-tails are also slightly larger than their immigrant cousins.

Nests are often frail structures of loosely arranged twigs, appearing at times to be incomplete and unable to hold the two white eggs. Nesting begins in May and the young will fly within six weeks. Large flocks may be found in early September in the regenerating forest lands surrounding the city, as they feed on salal berries prior to their southward migration.

WESTERN SCREECH-OWL

Otus kennicottii

larger than robin-sized

THE OWL THAT IS MOST likely to be seen and heard regularly in and around the city is the small Western Screech-Owl, which spends most of the daytime roosting. It is usually encountered at night when its call, a series of short, low notes which accelerate toward the end, gives away its presence. It calls throughout the year, but mostly during the breeding season from February to June. It is easily identified by its "ear" tufts, located outside and above its eyes.

Western Screech-Owls may be found in parks and other wooded areas, or even in quite densely populated areas provided there are enough large trees for cover and nesting. It lays its eggs in April in tree holes and cavities, often in old woodpecker holes — but it will also use nesting boxes erected in trees. This owl feeds on a wide variety of prey including insects, amphibians, fishes, worms, small mammals and birds. On occasion it will catch and kill prey larger than itself. Like many owls, it uses hearing to locate and catch food, but the prominent "ear" tufts have nothing to do with this: the real ears are located on the sides of the head.

More Western Screech-owls have been found on Victoria's Christmas Bird counts than elsewhere in the province.

GREAT HORNED OWL
Bubo virginianus
smaller than seagull-sized

THIS OWL IS THE MOST WIDESPREAD of all owls in North America. However, it is rarely seen by most people, except in a fleeting glimpse as it flies across a highway at night. It is a large bird, up to 65 cm long, and the female is larger than the male. Its ear tufts are much larger and farther apart than those of its smaller relative, the Western Screech-owl. The Great Horned Owl's large size, white throat and barred underparts are good identification features.

Great Horned Owls spend much of the day roosting in trees — usually near the trunks — and they do not seem to be put off by some human disturbance. Look for them in woodlands or isolated clumps of coniferous or deciduous trees. They are early nesters, laying their two eggs in late February in an abandoned hawk, crow or eagle nest.

They are powerful hunters and one of the few predators that will kill and eat animals the size of a raccoon. They usually eat a variety of small mammals and birds and swallow all but the larger prey items whole. The bones are regurgitated, wrapped in fur and feathers, as a pellet. Watch for these large pellets; they are a good clue to a roost or nest tree.

ANNA'S HUMMINGBIRD

Calypte anna

smaller than sparrow-sized

BRITISH COLUMBIA'S CAPITAL is fortunate to be a year-round home to North America's only non-migratory species of "hummer" — Anna's Hummingbird. This fascinating little gem first found its way onto southern Vancouver Island in about 1958. It is a bird of the Pacific Coast, most abundant in Southern California, and in Canada is found regularly only in the extreme southwestern part of British Columbia.

As in most birds, the iridescent colours of Anna's Hummingbird are produced, not by pigments, but by light waves refracting through the intricate structure of the feathers. Thus, by simply adjusting the angle and fit of his feathers, the male can turn on and off the brilliant rose-red signal lights of his head. In the "off" position, the gorget, or throat patch, appears almost black.

Look for this bird on the east side of the city — Gordon Head, Cadboro Bay and the university grounds. The males are highly territorial, often using the same perch every day of the year. Amazingly, this tiny bird will nest in the winter months; eggs may be laid as early as February and the young may be flying by April.

RUFOUS HUMMINGBIRD
Selasphorous rufus
smaller than sparrow-sized

DURING SUMMER, this is the common hummingbird of the city. The species migrates north in the spring to breed in western Canada, and British Columbia is the centre of its breeding range in North America. In the winter it migrates south to Mexico. It is hard to mistake a hummingbird: its small size, very rapid wing beats and bright colours are unique. The male Rufous Hummingbird is bright orange-rufous, with an iridescent throat patch or gorget. The female is whiter below, has a green back, rufous sides and lacks a gorget. It may be found in Victoria from early March to early October.

Hummingbirds will visit the back yard to feed on flower nectar, and are easily attracted to feeders filled with sugar water. It doesn't matter what colour the feeder solution is, but one half cup of white sugar dissolved in enough hot water to make one full cup of solution will keep them coming back.

Hummingbird nests are wonderful structures. They are less than 4 cm in diameter and made from mosses, lichens and plant down, held together with spider webs. Only two eggs are laid, usually between mid-May and mid-June. These are white and relatively large for the size of the birds. The incubation period is about 16 days and young can first fly when they are 21 days old.

BELTED KINGFISHER
Ceryle alcyon
larger than robin-sized

THIS BIG-HEADED, BLUE-GREY AND WHITE BIRD is a familar sight throughout Victoria. It dives headlong into the water to catch fish, sometimes from a perch 8 or 9 m high. The male has a blue band across the breast and the female is similar, but with a rufous band below the blue on the breast. Its rattling call is a good clue to its presence.

Belted Kingfishers feed on a variety of aquatic food: fish, frogs, tadpoles and insects. To see them, look near open water around the city; they feed in rivers, lakes and ponds, as well as along Victoria's shoreline and inner harbour. They like to fish from a perch overhanging the water, where they can see their prey moving below. They will frequently hover briefly before plunging bill-first into the water.

Kingfishers make their nests at the end of a burrow excavated in a river bank or sea cliff. The nests are particularly smelly once the young have hatched and the parents have started bringing fish to the young. Like many hole-nesting birds, their eggs are white. In many parts of Canada, kingfishers must migrate south when freeze-up locks out their food source, but here on the west coast they are resident throughout the year.

RED-BREASTED SAPSUCKER

Sphyrapicus ruber

smaller than robin-sized

IT IS HARD TO MISTAKE these colourful woodpeckers for any other species that occurs around the city. Both sexes have bright red heads and breasts, black backs and wings, a pale cream underside and white wing patches. Like all woodpeckers, they nest in holes that they excavate in tree trunks. They are rare in Victoria, but can be seen in woodlands at any time of the year and the neat rows of holes they màke in tree bark are a good clue to their presence.

Sapsuckers have evolved an interesting food gathering technique. Instead of boring into wood for insects and their larvae, they make shallow, almost square holes in the soft bark of trees, which then ooze the sap which these woodpeckers feed on. They are able to do this because their tongues are different from those of other woodpeckers. Most woodpeckers have long tongues, with barbs at the end to help them "spear" their prey. The Red-breasted Sapsucker has a shorter tongue, with brush-like bristles at the end to help it lap up sap. They also feed on insects attracted to the sap.

DOWNY WOODPECKER
Picoides pubescens
sparrow-sized

THE SMALLEST OF THE WOOD-PECKERS that you are likely to see in Victoria, the Downy Wood-pecker is about the same size as a sparrow. This is the most common of the woodpeckers to be seen around the city and can only be confused with the Hairy Wood-pecker, which is larger (about the size of a robin) and has a longer and thicker beak. The Downy Woodpecker has black wings mottled with white, a white back and underside and a black and white head. The male has a red patch on the back of his head.

If you want to attract them to a winter feeding station, try putting out suet in a plastic vegetable bag or simply hang it from a small branch. These woodpeckers seem to be very tolerant of people and are quite approachable when they are feeding. They nest in holes in trees, which they excavate with their beaks. During the breeding season, the males "drum" on trees — often using dead branches or power poles — which seem to amplify the sound. The Downy Woodpecker's "drum" sounds rather like a fast and prolonged drum roll. Drumming is a form of advertising territory, rather like singing in songbirds. Downy Woodpeckers also have a call, which is a rapid whinnying.

NORTHERN FLICKER

Colaptes auratus

larger than robin-sized

FOR A LONG TIME, it was thought that Red-shafted and Yellow-shafted Flickers were different species, the former found here, west of the Rockies, and the latter to the east of the Rockies. They are now known to be one species, the Northern Flicker. The phrase "red-shafted" refers to the colour of the feather quills of the flight feathers in the wings. Seen from below, these quills are red in the birds commonly found around the city. Probably the most widely noticed of the woodpeckers in this area, it is relatively large — a little smaller than a jay -- with a brown crown, grey face with a red mustache and a black and brown barred body. Its white rump is evident in flight. Unlike other woodpeckers, flickers are often seen feeding on the ground.

They excavate holes in trees for nesting cavities and these holes are often used by other species in subsequent breeding seasons. Birds such as bluebirds, American Kestrels, European Starlings, swallows and the smaller owls — even squirrels — use them. The holes are made in anything of wood, from dead trees to telephone poles and fence posts. They will even try wood on houses; that, combined with their early morning "drumming" on the noisiest thing they can find, such as a metal downpipe, have made them somewhat infamous.

OLIVE-SIDED FLYCATCHER

Contopus borealis

larger than sparrow-sized

THIS LARGE FLYCATCHER would be easily over-looked if it were not for its habit of perching near the tops of trees, and for its very distinctive call — *quick-three-beers* — which, once heard and recognized, is never forgotten. It has a typical upright flycatcher posture. The bird is olive-brown above, with white patches on either side of the rump, best seen when the bird flies. The breast has a pale central line separating the olive sides. The dark tail is comparatively short.

The Olive-sided Flycatcher is a summer visitor to the city, mainly from mid-May through August, and prefers coniferous woodlands and moist areas. It usually nests in a conifer, often high up on the end of a branch. It is particularly fond of perching in dead trees, from where it dashes out to catch insects. Listen for it in the spring on Mount Douglas or in the Highlands District near Francis-King Regional Park.

EURASIAN SKYLARK
Alauda arvensis
larger than sparrow-sized

FEW BIRDS CAN MATCH the Eurasian Skylark's outpourings of song for clarity and duration, and fewer still deliver such a thrilling sound from so high in the air. This bird advertises its presence and territory with continuous song for as long as eight minutes or more, all the time soaring high above its favourite habitat of large fields abandoned to the weeds and insects. The trills and warbles finally end with a headlong dive back down to earth.

Urban expansion has taken its toll on Victoria's farmland and, therefore, on North American's only resident skylark population. Perhaps as few as 100 birds remain where 1100 or more were present in the mid-sixties. One must now venture out to the Saanich Peninsula to hear and see this vocal sovereign. Search the weedy fields near the airport, Martindale Flats or the daffodil farms in Central Saanich. The male will occasionally burst into song in winter, but spring and summer are the best seasons to hear and see this distant relative of our native Horned Lark. When you hear his song, search high for a small speck of a bird, and then marvel at how he can maintain such a solo.

VIOLET-GREEN SWALLOW
Tachycineta thalassina
smaller than sparrow-sized

THIS SPECIES LOOKS VERY MUCH LIKE the Tree Swallow. Unlike its relative, though, the Violet-green Swallow has more white on the face, reaching above the eye, and white on its rump extending to its upper flanks. The Tree Swallow, on the other hand, has a metallic blue rump and back. Both species are among the earliest spring migrants to arrive in Victoria, the first individuals usually here by mid-February.

It is possible to attract Violet-green Swallows to your garden with suitable nesting boxes. They will take advantage of any appropriate hole or cavity; this might be a crevice high in a cliff, an old woodpecker hole or a hole in a building. They often nest in loose colonies, so it might be worthwhile to put up several boxes a few metres apart. They are often seen over water, where many swallows congregate to catch emerging aquatic insects. The Violet-green Swallow can be seen in the downtown core and inner harbour, flying erratically as it feeds above the trees and buildings.

BARN SWALLOW

Hirundo rustica

sparrow-sized

THE MOST NOTICEABLE FEATURE of the Barn Swallow is its deeply forked tail, which helps it to manoeuvre in flight while catching insects. Its back is uniformly blue and it has a deep red-brown throat, which fades into a cinnamon coloured breast. It is possible to tell the male and female apart by looking at the length of the tail. The male's tail is noticeably longer than the female's, which is only a little longer than the wings when she is at rest.

As its name suggests, the Barn Swallow is more than willing to associate with humans and their structures. Its preference for nesting in buildings, beneath bridges, and under the eaves of houses makes it a commonly seen swallow around the city, and a bird that we have all come to enjoy. It builds its nest from mud and grass collected from a nearby muddy spot. If a pair of swallows starts to build a nest on your property, try providing a wet patch from which they can collect mud; it is fascinating to watch them at close quarters. This species will sometimes raise two broods a year and when this happens, the first brood often helps the parents feed the second brood.

STELLER'S JAY

Cyanocitta stelleri

larger than robin-sized

THIS IS THE PROVINCIAL BIRD of British Columbia and, in Canada, is almost completely confined to this province. Perhaps the most noticeable feature of this very handsome bird is its large crest, which it raises and lowers at will. Steller's Jays are quite common in the outskirts of the city where there are plenty of trees. Members of the crow family seem to adapt quickly to humans, and jays are no exception: they have learned to associate people with food, and frequent back yards looking for scraps. They are a little shy at the feeder until they have become accustomed to it, but nevertheless, they come readily to food put out for them.

Steller's Jays usually nest in coniferous trees. The nest is substantial, if somewhat untidy, and is constructed with small sticks lined with mud, grass and roots. Three to five green-blue eggs, evenly spotted with dark brown, are laid. Jays are aggressive in the defence of their nests and will often drive off all but the most persistent intruders, letting the whole neighborhood know about it. They often drift into the city and residential yards in late autumn and winter, where they move from one feeding station to the next with a noisy *shack-shack-shack.*

Left: Inland Race
Right: Coastal Race

77

NORTHWESTERN CROW
Corvus caurinus
crow-sized

THIS IS THE CROW of the west coast, and is found only from northern Washington to the Aleutians in Alaska. It is a close relative of the American Crow, which is found throughout most of interior North America; however, it is smaller and has a lower *caw*. All crows seen around the city are Northwestern, as the range of the two species overlaps only on the mainland. They are the only medium-sized black birds to be found around the city. The Common Raven is larger, by a third.

Crows are renowned for taking advantage of changing circumstances and they have certainly adapted very well to people. One of the reasons that there are so many of them is because they quickly take advantage of humans' habit of leaving food around. Their abundance in Victoria, however, and all along the British Columbia coast, is a reflection of the plentiful food supply provided by the intertidal zone. The Northwestern Crow is a shoreline scavenger first and foremost.

It constructs a somewhat untidy nest of twigs, lined with grass and strips of bark, usually high in a conifer or boulevard tree. Four or five dull green eggs, blotched with dark brown, are laid.

COMMON RAVEN

Corvus corax

seagull-sized

THIS IS ONE OF OUR MOST EXCITING birds to watch. It is very clever, always on the move, and has many fascinating social traits. The raven is the largest member of the crow family, and is hard to confuse with any other species. When seen in flight, its tail is diamond-shaped. Its wide variety of calls includes a hoarse croak and sounds that are strangely unlike bird calls, almost bell-like. Not quite as bold around people as crows, ravens are still often seen around the city, particularly along the shore.

Ravens are found throughout most of Canada and in the northern regions of Europe and Asia. Although they nest on the ground in arctic situations, in Victoria they nest in very tall trees. Raven is featured in many west coast Indian stories and is often depicted in traditional art. One of the most exciting depictions of Raven and his association with people can be seen at the Museum of Anthropology at the University of British Columbia. Ravens take advantage of humans. In Victoria they work together to tip over garbage cans, steal food from pets, especially dogs, and pilfer corn, right from the cob, as it is growing in the fields.

CHESTNUT-BACKED CHICKADEE

Parus rufescens

smaller than sparrow-sized

THIS IS THE ONLY CHICKADEE on Vancouver Island. The most common chickadees throughout Canada are the Black-capped Chickadee and the browner Boreal Chickadee. The Chestnut-backed Chickadee has a brown cap, unlike the Black-capped Chickadee, and has red-brown on its back and sides. Chestnut-backed Chickadees are birds of coniferous forests, although they are also a common sight in any wooded park or back yard in the city. They frequent feeders, and are particularly fond of sunflower seeds and suet.

Normally they nest in tree cavities which they often excavate themselves in very soft wood. They will also use holes of other birds such as Downy Woodpeckers, as well as natural cavities. A birdhouse is good substitute. To ensure that sparrows do not take the box over, make your house with an opening of 32 mm (sparrows need 38 mm). Commercial bird houses may be adapted by gluing pieces of wood with the correctly sized opening over the existing hole.

BUSHTIT
Psaltriparus minimus
smaller than sparrow-sized

THE CHARACTER OF THE HOME reflects the quality of the occupant, and the tiny grey Bushtit sets a fine example. The architecture of its nest is worth a close look. Intricate weaving of fine fibres, spider webs, grasses, mosses and lichens results in what one might mistake for an old gray sock hanging from a bushy shrub. A three-centimetre entrance hole is set high on one side, allowing both parents access, yet retaining total concealment of the five or six tiny white eggs or young. This little bird, with its long, floppy tail, is a masterful weaver.

Winter flocks of 15 to 30 move haltingly through the mixed shrubs and trees, hanging upside down or sideways as they search for insect eggs and larvae. They remain in touch with one another more by sound than by sight, their drab bodies and grey-brown heads blending with the shrubbery. Soft, lisping seeps and twitters are often heard before the birds are seen.

Bushtits are a favourite feeder visitor. Beef suet hanging from a flimsy branch (to frustrate crows and starlings) will result in repeated visits from local families of Bushtits. They crowd onto the fat like a swarm of bees. It is then that one can approach for a close-up view.

RED-BREASTED NUTHATCH
Sitta canadensis
smaller than sparrow-sized

NUTHATCHES HAVE A VERY DISTINCTIVE SHAPE and the strange habit of moving head-down as they feed from the upper to the lower parts of a tree. These are probably the best clues to their identification. They may have evolved this feeding strategy to exploit the bark of trees from an angle which increases the likelihood of their finding food that other birds have missed.

Red-breasted Nuthatches are rare nesters within the city but they will come readily to feeders, where they like sunflower seeds and suet. Usually they are found high up in stands of coniferous trees and mixed woodlands, although they will also feed in the Garry oaks and other deciduous trees.

Nuthatches nest in holes in trees, which they sometimes excavate themselves, although they also use natural cavities and old woodpecker holes. Red-breasted Nuthatches have an interesting habit of smearing pitch or mud around the entrances to their nest-holes. Why they do this is uncertain, but it may serve to reinforce the entrance against predators such as squirrels and woodpeckers, and by reducing the size of the entrance it may prevent larger birds from getting in.

BEWICK'S WREN
Thryomanes bewickii
smaller than sparrow-sized

THIS IS THE MOST COMMON back yard wren of Victoria. Typical of all wrens, it often cocks its tail over its back, displaying bold brown and white barring. A distinctive white eye-line and whitish underparts separate this species from its closest relative, the House Wren, which also nests here.

Bewick's Wren can be heard year-round uttering a series of clear, sharp notes, often preceded by a buzzy rasp. When alarmed, it alerts other birds by approaching the intruder and scolding noisily. In fact, an effective way of attracting this and many other species is to "squeak" with a kissing or hissing sound to simulate a bird in distress. With practice you may find yourself surrounded by a group of curious and agitated birds, many of which you had no idea were nearby.

Nest sites selected by this insect-eater are sometimes bizarre and imaginative. Wood piles, old jars or baskets tucked away at the back of a shed, electrical fuse boxes and even abandoned wasps' nests may serve as a secure place to raise young ones. Most often, though, a natural cavity in a tree or a small nest box will be used.

WINTER WREN
Troglodytes troglodytes
smaller than sparrow-sized

MORE OFTEN HEARD THAN SEEN, the Winter Wren has a long explosive song which is out of proportion to the size of the bird. It usually sings its series of musical trills from dense cover. This dark brown bird is small, only 10 cm in length, with a short stubby tail which is often carried cocked over its back. When seen at close quarters, its plumage is beautifully barred, the underside paler than the back. In winter, look and listen for it low down in thick, moist, damp woodlands of the city, but watch for it also in the garden if you have an overgrown corner with thick vegetation.

Its scientific name, *Troglodytes*, is most apt. It means "cave dweller" in Greek and, while nesting, the Winter Wren is just that. The male constructs a number of nests for the female to choose from. Each is an elaborate structure of leaves, mosses, grasses and other plant material in the shape of a ball, with a small entrance hole in the side. The nest is usually tucked away in the roots of an upturned tree or under the bank of a stream.

AMERICAN DIPPER
Cinclus mexicanus
larger than sparrow-sized

THIS IS AN EXCITING BIRD to watch. Looking rather like a large fat wren, it is almost uniformly grey and about the size of a European Starling. It is found exclusively beside fast-flowing streams, so a short excursion from the centre of the city will be necessary. There is an excellent chance of seeing this bird beside the Goldstream River in Goldstream Provincial Park, or at Sooke Potholes on the Sooke River.

American Dippers feed on small aquatic invertebrates and small fishes. To watch a dipper feeding is fascinating, as they frequently search for food below the surface. They do this by wading or diving into the water and then bobbing underneath, where they remain for some time before popping up again. While under water, they actively seek out their prey while walking along the bottom of the stream. Another characteristic to watch for is their constant bobbing up and down, as if the whole bird were on springs. Dippers are often quite hard to spot; the first indication of their presence is likely to be either their loud bubbling song, or a blur of grey as they fly past on their way up or down the river.

GOLDEN-CROWNED KINGLET

Regulus satrapa
smaller than sparrow-sized

RUBY-CROWNED KINGLET

Regulus calendula
smaller than sparrow-sized

THE GOLDEN-CROWNED KINGLET is a small, plump (10 cm long), olive-green bird, most noticeable for a bright crown edged in black and white; the male's is a combination of orange and yellow feathers, giving the impression of bright gold; the female's is a uniform bright yellow. Like its nearest relative, the Ruby-crowned Kinglet, these birds have two white wing-bars and a habit of nervously flicking their wings as they feed. The best way to tell the two apart is to look for the white eyebrow, striped crown and the light belly on the Golden-crown. The Ruby-crown is a more evenly-coloured olive-green all over and has a prominent white eye ring. Its striking red crown (male only) is seen only during courtship and aggression.

The Golden-crowned Kinglet is a resident bird wherever coniferous or mixed woodlands occur. Its voice is a very high pitched *tsee-tsee-tsee*, so high in fact that it is outside the hearing range of some people.

The Ruby-crowned Kinglet is an autumn to spring visitor, moving north and inland to breed. March and April are the best months to see it here, in mixed deciduous habitats, often in company with small flocks of Golden-crowns. Its surprisingly loud song of up-slurred whistled phrases is the best clue to its presence.

Top: Golden-crowned Kinglet
Bottom: Ruby-crowned Kinglet

AMERICAN ROBIN
Turdus migratorius
robin-sized

A ROBIN'S SONG is perhaps the best reminder that spring is starting. This, the best known of city birds, is a good example of how well some creatures adapt to the human environment. The robin is really a forest bird, found whereever there is suitable woodland with clearings — from the tree limit in the north and south across all of Canada. The cities provide a wonderful habitat with their hedgerows, large trees to nest in and plenty of short grassy areas in which to hunt for earthworms and insect larvae. Berries, apples and small fruits are a favorite winter food.

The males sing from house tops, trees and telephone wires to define their territories, and it is not unusual to see two males fighting on the ground in a territorial dispute. The birds nest in trees and in suitable recesses in buildings, where they build a sturdy nest of plant stems and coarse grass lined with mud and fine grass. The eggs are pale blue and it is not unusual to find an eggshell on the ground during the spring or summer. If it is chipped neatly in half around the middle, the egg has probably just hatched and the shell been disposed of by a parent.

VARIED THRUSH

Ixoreus naevius

robin-sized

ONE OF THE MOST EVOCATIVE SOUNDS of nature is the song of a Varied Thrush. Its call is a series of unhurried single notes, each of them slightly higher or lower in pitch than its predecessor. This thrush usually sings from cover or high in a tree, and its song is the best clue to its presence. It is a very retiring bird and not always easy to spot. Persevere, as it is a lovely bird to see, a subtle mixture of blue-grey, black and orange. The black chest-band is diagnostic. It is very much a bird of the forest and it is found throughout much of the province where there is suitable cover.

The best time to see this bird in Victoria is during the rare cold spells of winter, when snows blanket the surrounding hills. At this time, the birds leave the forest and start to forage in any suitable areas, including residential gardens. They can then be seen in the open more often and may even feed on the ground under a back yard feeder.

89

CEDAR WAXWING

Bombycilla cedrorum

larger than sparrow-sized

THIS HANDSOME BIRD can be seen at any time of the year in and around the city, but is most common from June to October. It has an overall sleek appearance, with a very smooth-looking plumage. Red wax-like extensions of the secondary wing feathers give the bird its name. Cedar Waxwings can be found along the edges of most wooded habitats, whether open forest, city parks or the back yard. Except during the breeding season when they pair off, waxwings spend most of their time in flocks; towards the end of winter these flocks can become quite large. This is a good strategy against predators, such as the Merlin and Cooper's Hawk: flocking often confuses a predator and gives the individual a better chance to get away. Most important, many eyes are better than a single pair for detecting a predator.

This bird nests out on the branch of a tree or bush. The nest is constructed from a wide variety of materials, depending on what is available — an assortment of plant matter including lichens and roots may be used, along with paper, dog hair, twine and whatever else can be found. They lay blue-grey eggs, which are spotted with black or brown.

EUROPEAN STARLING

Sturnus vulgaris

smaller than robin-sized

THIS STUBBY BLACK BIRD is a familiar sight in the city, a truly urban bird that is here year round. The first starlings were brought to New York from Europe in 1890; they have since spread rapidly and are now common over most of North America.

Starlings are really woodland-edge birds, but they are remarkably adaptable and their principal needs are a supply of suitable nesting holes and plenty of nearby grassy areas in which to feed. They nest in old woodpecker holes or in a broken tree branch, but they are just as much at home under the eaves of a house. They find the well cut grass of back yards, golf courses and city parks to their liking, and they do an immense amount of good, feeding on insect grubs. They also appreciate bird feeders.

Starlings are wonderful mimics and incorporate snatches of other birds' songs into their own, Killdeer calls seeming to be a favourite. They also imitate many city noises, including the squeak of garage doors and dog whistles. Although some starlings fly south in the winter, others stay, and on colder days they often huddle over a chimney to keep warm. At night, they roost together in immense flocks on city buildings, bridges or in boulevard trees.

ORANGE-CROWNED WARBLER

Vermivora celata
smaller than sparrow-sized

THIS BIRD IS NOTICEABLE by its lack of field characteristics. It is a yellow-green warbler, slightly paler below, and the male's dusky orange crown is almost impossible to see unless the bird is handled or seen at close range in good light. It is a common nesting species in open deciduous woodland and along the woodland edges around the city. Even its call is somewhat indistinct until you have heard it a few times. It is best described as a single, slightly descending trill.

YELLOW-RUMPED WARBLER

Dendroica coronata
smaller than sparrow-sized

FOR MANY YEARS, the two different colour variations of the Yellow-rumped Warbler were treated as separate species, the Myrtle Warbler of the east and Audubon's Warbler of the west. Today, they are known to be one species. It is probably Canada's most common warbler, breeding over most of the country, except in the high Arctic and the Canadian shield.

Both subspecies can be seen here in the city during migration, although Audubon's race is the common nesting form. Its throat, shoulder and crown are yellow, while the rest of the bird is a patterned mixture of blacks, whites and blue-greys. The throat in the Myrtle Warbler is yellow. Unlike most of our warblers, the Yellow-rumped Warbler will overwinter in small numbers on the west coast, particularly around Swan Lake and moist shoreline areas. During the summer months, warblers feed on small insects; during the winter when there are far fewer insects about, the Yellow-rumped Warbler will eat small berries.

The birds make a loosely constructed and rather untidy nest of roots, grass, and small twigs, lined with soft material. They normally build their nests in a conifer, a few metres from the ground.

Top: Orange-crowned Warbler
Bottom: Yellow-rumped Warbler

93

COMMON YELLOWTHROAT
Geothlypis trichas
smaller than sparrow-sized

THE MALE COMMON YELLOWTHROAT is striking, and is easily identified by his broad black "robber's" mask that extends well behind the eyes. The back is olive green and the throat, breast and undersides are bright yellow. The female looks somewhat like the male, but lacks the black mask and brightness of colour. These active birds are found in shrubby areas, almost always near water, and they are most common in cattail beds. Listen for the distinctive call, *witchety-witchety-witchety*, as this is the best clue to the Yellowthroat's presence. It should be found at Quick's Bottom and Swan Lake from April through September.

WILSON'S WARBLER
Wilsonia pusilla
smaller than sparrow-sized

WILSON'S WARBLER is one of the more common warblers of this part of British Columbia. It is a strikingly bright yellow on the head, breast and underparts and on the top of the male's head is a small black cap, which can be very hard to see if the bird is above you or is moving about in the vegetation. The back, tail and wings are olive green. The bird is most common in damp places, in fairly thick vegetation. Look for it around ponds, bogs and along stream banks. On migration in the fall and spring, it can be found almost anywhere, even in back yards.

WESTERN TANAGER
Piranga ludoviciana
larger than sparrow-sized

THIS SUMMER VISITOR to the province is a bird of open forests. In Victoria it is most common in May as it moves northward. It may be found in many of the woodlands around the city, as well as in the larger parks, so long as there are plenty of large mature trees. The male is a very attractive bird, washed in red on the head, with a bright yellow body contrasting with black wings and tail. It has very noticeable yellow wing bars, which can be useful in identifying the bird. The female is much less brightly marked, with an olive back and tail, and a pale yellow underside.

Western Tanagers construct an untidy nest of twigs and grass, often in a coniferous tree. The young birds look very much like the rather drab female once they have fledged. In the fall the birds move south to winter in Central America.

BLACK-HEADED GROSBEAK
Pheucticus melanocephalus
smaller than robin-sized

GROSBEAKS ARE CHARACTERIZED by their large, powerful beaks. The male Black-headed Grosbeak shows a vastly different plumage than the female. He has a cinnamon-brown breast, and black head, back, wings and tail. The wings have two white bars on them — about the only similarity between the sexes. The female is a much more drab, mottled brown.

Grosbeaks tend to be birds of mature deciduous woodland with plenty of shrubby growth below the trees. Typical habitats would be beside lakes, in older mixed forests and alongside streams and rivers. They find this sort of habitat near Blenkinsop Lake and occasionally in larger, more mature back yards. They nest in trees or bushes and build an untidy and seemingly badly made nest, in which they lay three or four pale blue eggs spotted with brown. The males share the incubating and have a habit peculiar to grosbeaks of singing on the nest. The warblings are somewhat similar to those of the American Robin, but are more clipped and harsh.

RUFOUS-SIDED TOWHEE
Pipilo erythrophthalmus
smaller than robin-sized

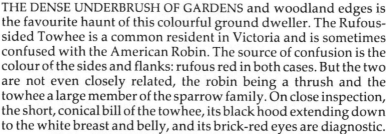

THE DENSE UNDERBRUSH OF GARDENS and woodland edges is the favourite haunt of this colourful ground dweller. The Rufous-sided Towhee is a common resident in Victoria and is sometimes confused with the American Robin. The source of confusion is the colour of the sides and flanks: rufous red in both cases. But the two are not even closely related, the robin being a thrush and the towhee a large member of the sparrow family. On close inspection, the short, conical bill of the towhee, its black hood extending down to the white breast and belly, and its brick-red eyes are diagnostic.

A stroll through Uplands Park or along a powerline clearing will invariably evoke a questioning note from the Rufous-sided Towhee — a nasal, up-slurred *Wheer?* as if to ask "Who goes there?" The song includes repeated phrases, often ending with a sharp trill.

The nest is usually close to the ground, well hidden in the base of a thicket or a garden shrub that has trapped a few of last year's fallen leaves. Grubs and insects make up most of the diet of young birds, but seeds are important through the winter. This bird is a regular visitor to feeders, preferring to feed on seeds spilled to the ground.

FOX SPARROW
Passerella iliaca
sparrow-sized

THE FOX SPARROW can be told from the Song Sparrow by its uniformly dark head and the lack of streaks on the upper parts. It is a large sparrow, with a dark sooty brown head, back and wings. Its breast is pale, with dark streaking well down to the underside. The song is musical and short, a series of two or three slurred notes followed by a series of shorter, quicker notes. In Victoria, it is heard only in the spring, just prior to its departure northward to the higher forests to nest.

It is found in thickets and scrubby woodland, and can often be seen in urban areas on land that has been cleared and has a dense regrowth of shrubs and brambles. It often finds its way into the back yard in winter, particularly if there is a suitably neglected area and a feeder full of seeds. It is a variable species, with many different plumages throughout Canada. The subspecies found here on the west coast of British Columbia is very dark, but in the north, the red-brown (fox-coloured) subspecies that gives the sparrow its name, is the common form.

SONG SPARROW
Melospiza melodia
sparrow-sized

PERHAPS THE MOST OBVIOUS FEATURE of the Song Sparrow is its long rounded tail. Even when the bird flies, this is one of its most distinctive features, as is the way the bird pumps its tail in flight. The back and wings are a dark, sooty brown. The head is streaked with grey, and the brown streaking of the breast often forms a dark spot in the centre. The Song Sparrow has a very pleasant song which begins with a series of two or three loud notes that are followed by a buzzy call and a trill; listen for it in the spring and summer.

The Song Sparrow is a bird that inhabits bushy shrubbery on the edges of woodland or beside streams, lakes and the seashore, away from the heavily urbanized areas of the city. Our gardens can often provide just such a habitat, and Song Sparrows are frequently found in gardens that have thick shrubbery or a neglected corner. They will also make use of hedges, which provide suitable nesting sites. A feeder containing mixed seeds will usually attract a Song Sparrow or two for the winter.

DARK-EYED JUNCO

Junco hyemalis

sparrow-sized

UNTIL ABOUT FIFTEEN YEARS AGO, the "Oregon Junco" and the "Slate-coloured Junco" were considered two of a number of different species of junco, all of which are now recognized as belonging to the same species, the Dark-eyed Junco. The subspecies vary considerably throughout North America and the form most common here, the "Oregon," is perhaps the most attractive. The male and the female look alike, except that the female lacks the jet black hood of the male and has, instead, a dark grey hood.

These birds are seen in the back yard quite commonly — particularly during the fall and winter months when they spend a considerable amount of time at the edges of bushes hunting for food on the ground, or at a feeder. In the breeding season, they tend to frequent the edges of coniferous woodland, and a well-treed back yard makes a good substitute. They build their nests on the ground, usually well concealed in the vegetation, or in suitable holes and hollows on or very near the ground. They lay four or five white, speckled eggs.

RED-WINGED BLACKBIRD

Agelaius phoeniceus
smaller than robin-sized

THE CALL OF THE RED-WINGED BLACKBIRD in the spring announces the change of season. The male birds are hard to miss with their bright red wing patches, which they use to warn off males from adjoining territories. The size and intensity of colour of the wing patch and the way the bird uses it during his display is directly related to how successful the male is in attracting a mate, or group of females, which will nest in his territory. The female, by contrast, is far less conspicuous and at first glance would appear to belong to a completely different species. She is a heavily striped, brown bird with a marked buff streak over the eye.

Look for them in wet areas beside ponds, lakes and along the banks of slow-moving rivers, where they often nest in loose colonies. The colonies are very noisy with the distinctive *onk-aa-ree-a* call of the males and their frequent territorial disputes. The rough-grass nests are often built on two or more cattail stalks over water. The birds are present year-round in suitable habitats near the city, but their numbers swell in the spring as more birds arrive from their southern wintering grounds.

NORTHERN ORIOLE

Icterus galbula

smaller than robin-sized

THE NORTHERN ORIOLE is not common around the city, or on the west coast, although it breeds commonly in the south-central part of British Columbia and less regularly out to the west coast, including greater Victoria. This species differs in colour a great deal between the east and the west of the continent: for a long time it was thought that two species existed, the eastern Baltimore Oriole, and Bullock's Oriole in the west. The male Bullock's is handsome, with an orange body, black bib, crown and tail and black and white wings. By contrast, the female is pale olive. It is hard to spot orioles as they spend a good deal of their time high in the tree canopy. The male's rich flutey song usually gives his presence away long before he is sighted.

Orioles build intriguing hanging nests, which they suspend from a branch. They use a variety of materials, which they weave into a very strong construction. The nests remain for some time and are frequently built in poplar or other deciduous trees, where they are often visible the following winter. Orioles are unusual in their liking for hairy caterpillars which most birds go out of their way to avoid.

PURPLE FINCH
Carpodacus purpureus
smaller than sparrow-sized

HOUSE FINCH
Carpodacus mexicanus
smaller than sparrow-sized

THE PURPLE FINCH is most commonly seen around the city during the winter months. It is a frequent visitor to the bird feeder, seeking small seeds which it shells with its relatively large beak. Watch for a sparrow-sized bird. The male has a purple-red head and breast, while the female is much less gaudy, with an olive-brown back and streaked head and breast. Like all finches, they have a slightly forked tail, which is particularly noticeable in flight. Their call is a distinctive *pic*.

The House Finch is a common city bird year round. The red on the breast, head and rump of the male lacks the purplish tones of the Purple Finch and does not extend to the back. The female is uniformly grey with light striping and no light eyeline.

Purple Finches inhabit open areas on the edges of woodland. They build a nest of roots, grass and small sticks and line it with soft material. The nest is normally in a coniferous tree, but is sometimes located in the garden in a suitably dense hedge. House Finches nest in city parks and gardens, often around the vine-covered buildings in the heart of the city.

Purple Finch

RED CROSSBILL
Loxia curvirostra
sparrow-sized

AS THE NAME SUGGESTS, crossbills have a unique beak, with the large upper mandible crossing over the lower mandible. This looks awkward until you see the birds using their beaks to extract the seeds of conifer cones; the perfection of the shape then becomes obvious. The Red Crossbill is a medium-sized finch (16 cm in length). The males have a red head and breast and a red-brown back. The females are yellow and brown and the young are mottled on the breast and head, with a brown back and wings.

This species is highly irregular in its distribution. In some years it is very common in coniferous woodland around the city, but if it is a poor year for coniferous seed cone production, the birds move elsewhere. The crossbill is unusual in that it breeds at almost any time of the year. The birds move about in loose flocks and the *jip-jip* calls and the remains of cones on the ground are good indications of their presence. Watch also for the White-winged Crossbill, which is rare here on the coast but common in the interior of the province. It looks similar, but has two very obvious white wing bars.

PINE SISKIN
Carduelis pinus
smaller than sparrow-sized

THIS SMALL FINCH is seen in large flocks or small groups. It may even breed in loose colonies. Pine Siskins will often visit a feeder, particularly a hanging feeder, if it is stocked with small seeds. They are the most acrobatic of the finches and, like the chickadees, will feed while upside down on an alder or fir twig. Watch for a pale brown, heavily streaked finch, with some dull yellow on the wings and tail. This yellow is much more noticeable when the birds fly. Like all finches, the Pine Siskin has a forked tail, also more noticeable in flight.

It has a very distinctive call, a good clue to its presence, which sounds like a slightly harsh *zwee-e-e-e-t?* Birds in a flock give this call frequently. A flock of siskins is very active and moves through the trees quite quickly, looking for food. They are predominantly seed eaters, but they also forage for small insects hidden in crevices in the bark. In the early spring they also feed on buds.

AMERICAN GOLDFINCH
Carduelis tristis
smaller than sparrow-sized

IN THE BREEDING SEASON, the male American Goldfinch is a very handsome bird — a bright sulphur yellow, offset with a black cap, wings and tail. The female is a more subdued olive yellow and she lacks the black cap. In the winter, the birds look somewhat different, the yellow being replaced by a more unobtrusive brown. The birds still show their black wings and tail and the male especially has a little yellow on the throat.

These are seed-eating birds and if you know the location of a large patch of thistles, you will be almost certain to see goldfinches around the plants in the late summer, as they perch on the tops of the seed heads, feeding on the minute thistle seeds. They prefer open places, with trees nearby. A patch of waste ground around the city, or a neglected field, are suitable habitats. They build a cup-shaped nest in trees, of grass and other plant material which they line with plant down. Their four to six eggs are pale blue.

107

EVENING GROSBEAK
Coccothraustes vespertinus

larger than sparrow-sized

MOST COMMONLY SEEN around the city in flocks during the spring, the Evening Grosbeak feeds on moth larvae, other arboreal insects and last year's berries and seeds. However it is not very far away in winter and summer. The movements of the Evening Grosbeak are confusing. Some seem to "disappear" into coniferous or mixed forest, while others may migrate out of the province.

In the fall, the Evening Grosbeaks start to flock and at this time they enter more populated areas around the city. They are readily tempted to the feeder with sunflowers seeds, which they easily crack open with their large bills. The plumage is elegant: a yellow body, black wings, tail and cap and a brown head and neck. The female is buff-coloured instead of yellow and both sexes show a white wing patch in flight. The female Pine Grosbeak is somewhat similar, but Pine Grosbeaks are rare in Victoria and have black beaks and legs and lack the broad white wing patch. Listen for the piercing call of the Evening Grosbeak as they communicate to keep the flock together.

HOUSE SPARROW

Passer domesticus

sparrow-sized

WHILE WE OFTEN REGARD SPARROWS as pesky nuisances, they are very much a part of city life. Their noisy song is a series of very monotonous *chirrups*, memorable only for the enthusiasm with which it is delivered!

Outside the breeding season, House Sparrows are often seen in small flocks in both urban and rural areas. They seem to survive well wherever there is human settlement, even downtown. The species is not native to this continent, but was first introduced in the 1850s, ostensibly to help control insect pests. Since then, it has spread to the whole of the continent south of the 60th parallel.

Sparrows are cavity-nesting birds and their adaptability and ingenuity have allowed them to make good use of buildings. They are especially fond of bird houses and will often take over those put up to attract other species, provided the holes are large enough for them: at least 38 mm in diameter. They start breeding in early spring and often have more than one brood. At the feeder, particularly the tray type, they often dominate. It is less easy for them to chase other birds away at hanging feeders.

ATTRACTING BIRDS

GETTING STARTED AT BIRDWATCHING need not cost a lot of money. Many people derive a great deal of pleasure by simply putting out household scraps for birds on a homemade feeder, close enough to the window that birds can be seen as they come and go.

It is certainly not necessary to be able to identify all the birds at the feeder to be able to enjoy them, but there is a great sense of satisfaction in being able to tell one species from another. Human nature being what it is, we tend to want to learn.

Most people interested in watching birds use binoculars, as this allows them to identify key characteristics such as plumage, leg colour, and bill shape. Binoculars also allow the user to watch the more timid birds that normally stay at a distance, or remain in the cover of bushes and trees, and allow us to study birds' behaviour. Small details help to build the overall picture of a bird, which helps to identify the species.

An attractive back yard offers many birdwatching opportunities.

Buying binoculars is perhaps the biggest financial outlay the birdwatcher will make, but it is not necessary to spend a great deal of money as there are many inexpensive but good models. Buying binoculars can be confusing, and much has been written about how to choose a pair. The best advice is to ask a birdwatcher or to talk to someone at a local nature centre. Remember that no one pair will be perfect for every situation — watching birds in woodland requires binoculars with a wide field of view but a reasonably low magnification (8X would be ideal), whereas watching shorebirds in an estuary would require a higher magnification, and a telescope would then be useful. Binoculars tend to get heavy around the neck, and it is a good idea to keep this in mind when selecting the right pair. A wider neck strap certainly helps, but if you have a choice, you will not regret going for the lightest pair that seems to be right for you.

Aside from binoculars, the only other piece of equipment needed is a book that will enable you to identify the birds you see. Armed with a pair of binoculars and a good field guide, you will find a whole new world opening up for you as you take advantage of the many excellent birdwatching sites in and around the city, or enjoy your own back yard birds more.

Soon, you will be taking your binoculars with you on a hike or as you take the dog for a walk in the park — the opportunities for their use are endless.

Birds are easily viewed in their natural habitat through binoculars.

BIRD FEEDERS

Why bother with a bird feeder in your back yard? The great advantage is that by feeding birds on a regular basis, they learn to come to that spot every day and as more birds learn, the numbers of species and individuals increase. Your back yard can become your own bird sanctuary.

Feeders also provide advantages for birds. They are used much more frequently when their natural food sources are less abundant — particularly in the winter months. Here on the west coast, we rarely have spells of harsh weather, but when it does get colder, the birds using the neighbourhood feeders may rely on this food source for survival. Once feeding is started, it should be maintained throughout the winter and particularly during the colder weather. A break in the normal routine could well mean that the birds you have so carefully attracted will move on or, if the weather is unusually bitter, may not survive. Try feeding the birds at the same time each day and you will notice how they quickly adjust to a daily routine. Early morning is best. Better still, provide sufficient food to last two or three days.

There may only be a few birds at the feeder at any one time, but this does not necessarily mean that only a few birds are using the feeder. It can be difficult to recognize individuals, but by banding and watching them as they come back to feeders, it has been shown that birds use feeders for only short periods during the day. Any one feeder may be visited by many individuals throughout the daylight hours as they forage through the neighbourhood. This is normal, particularly in the winter when they must range over a much wider area to find the variety of foods they need to sustain themselves.

Steller's Jays feeding at a tray feeder.

Chestnut-backed chickadees at a seed dispenser.

When you place a feeder in the garden, don't expect the birds to find it immediately. It often takes a few weeks for numbers to build up, so persevere and be patient.

It is best to position the feeder some distance from the house, as the birds will be wary if they see movement. Find a site that is likely to be attractive to birds: immediately adjacent to dense trees or bushes for instance, rather than in the centre of the lawn. Immediate escape cover is as important as the food itself. Small birds are innately aware of the danger of avian predators — Cooper's Hawks, Sharp-shinned Hawks and Merlins — and will soon take a liking to a feeder that offers safety as well as good fare.

Bear in mind also that cats can be a real threat, so make it difficult for them by ensuring that the birds have a chance to see them. Avoid positioning your feeder right beside a suitable hiding place, such as a low bush, and make sure that it is high enough to be out of reach of the agile cat — which can leap as high as two metres. A large circle of page wire under the feeder will soon dissuade the neighbour's Tabby.

There are countless designs for bird feeders, but essentially they all do exactly the same job: they dispense food that birds will eat in a convenient and hygienic manner. Depending on the type of birds one wishes to attract, there are four basic designs:

- hanging seed dispensers for birdseed
- tray feeders for mixed bird foods
- suet feeders
- hummingbird feeders

114

Hanging Seed Dispensers

These come in many different designs, but if you bear a few points in mind it is easy to select the right one.

The feeder should be large enough to hold a good supply of seeds; otherwise, you will be forever refilling it. The ease with which the feeder can be filled is also important. Birds will eat most during the coldest periods, so you'll need a feeder that is easy to open and close on a cold day.

All feeders should be cleaned regularly so they should be easy to take apart. The seed should be protected from the rain and snow. Clear plastic seed containers are the best — they clean easily, are reasonably strong, allow you to see when they need refilling, and allow the birds to see what is inside them.

There are many commercial seed mixtures available for hanging feeders, but a surprising number of birds seem to prefer sunflower seeds: if you put up two feeders, one with a mixture and one with sunflower seeds, you will be able to observe the preferences yourself.

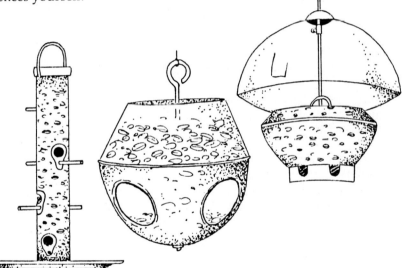

LEFT: A simple seed dispenser, well designed with perches for birds and a feeding tray at the bottom. Very attractive to the chestnut-backed chickadees.
CENTRE: A larger seed dispenser that holds more food and has larger openings to allow bigger birds to use it.
RIGHT: A seed hopper with a plastic dome that keeps off squirrels and larger birds. It has good seed capability and is ideal for smaller birds.

Tray Feeders

This type of feeder can be designed to attract many different types of birds, from seed eaters to those that forage on the ground. Some tray feeders have a hopper, with the tray immediately below to catch the seed and provide a feeding area. These work well, but have some disadvantages. There is never enough room for all the birds to feed without overcrowding, and so the more dominant species and individuals tend to drive others away. It is also quite difficult to see the birds at the feeder. The more timid ones tend to feed on the side furthest from your sight —a problem which can be overcome if you arrange to have only one outlet.

Perhaps the best type of tray feeders are those that are nothing more than a large tray, onto which seed and other scraps are spread. It should have a lip to stop too much food from spilling or blowing onto the ground. But don't worry about the spillage; you will find that many species prefer to feed on the ground under the feeder. Position this type of feeder near some dense tree or shrub cover. And again, a temporary wire fence with at least 10 cm mesh will keep the cat from lunging directly under the feeder, yet will allow casual access for birds as large as California Quail.

Suet Feeders

You can get beef suet from the meat counter at the supermarket and birds such as woodpeckers, chickadees and Bushtits love it. It is a good high-energy food for birds in cold weather and is easy to feed as it comes in a lump, lasts a while, and can be simply suspended in an old onion bag or from a string. Other types of suet feeders can be made using wire mesh: the plastic-coated type is best, as birds can damage themselves on normal metal mesh especially in cold weather. If you have the tools, bore holes in a short log and push suet into the holes, then hang this up.

A tray-type feeder with a hopper that has see-through sides for easy checking of food levels.

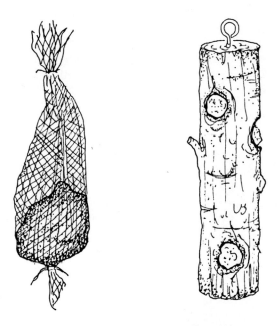

LEFT: *The simplest of all suet dispensers: an old onion bag, easily replaceable.*
RIGHT: *A more natural type of suet dispenser: an old log with holes drilled in it and stuffed with suet.*

Hummingbird Feeders

Although the Rufous Hummingbird is the species that is most common on the west coast, Anna's Hummingbird is also found in the area in increasing numbers, so watch for both species. It is possible to attract them into your garden with a colourful variety of flowers, but a good hummingbird feeder is one of the best ways to keep them coming back. When buying a feeder, look closely at the seals that keep the fluid in the container and choose one that looks well made. Most of them work, but the cheaper ones don't last long and frequently drip. This attracts wasps, bees and ants and leaves the feeder empty in short order. A hummingbird feeder should have some red on it, as this helps to attract the birds. You can make your own feeding fluid by dissolving two to three parts of white sugar in one to three parts of near-boiling water. Experiment and see what concentration seems to be preferred. There is no need to add red dye to the liquid, and never use honey as this ferments readily and may grow a mold that can be fatal to hummingbirds. It is important to clean the feeder frequently. In warm weather, add only a bit of liquid each time and let your feathered visitors consume it before it ferments. Keep the refill jar in the refrigerator.

Because hummingbirds are so small, it is most rewarding to hang the feeder near a window, or on the deck, where the birds quickly become accustomed to people and will allow you to watch at close range.

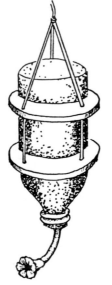

A home-made hummingbird feeder. Use an artificial red flower at the mouth.

Nest Boxes

Different species of birds have evolved to take advantage of different habitats. Each species uses a different feeding strategy and a different nesting strategy. By providing a variety of different types of food at your feeder, it is possible to attract ground-feeding birds and tree-feeding birds, seed eaters, omnivorous birds and even the odd bird of prey. The same is true if one provides a variety of different nesting opportunities. Birds will be attracted to artificial sites during the breeding season. Although some boxes may not be used the first year, they can be relocated next season.

There are many misconceptions about nest boxes. For example, birds don't need a perch on the front of the bird house — a perch is most useful for predators such as starlings that are trying to steal eggs or young. Although you may appreciate rounded corners on a bird house and a well-sanded exterior, birds prefer rough wood and a natural look. At the end of the season, clean the nest box out. This helps to prevent nest parasites from over-wintering, and

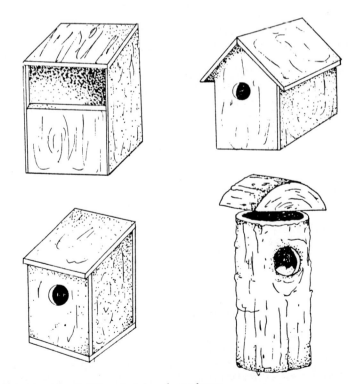

A few examples of different styles of nest boxes.

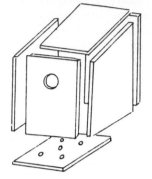

The construction of a nest box from a plank of wood.

gives birds a vacant box for the following spring. Don't disturb the house when it's in use as you may cause the adults to desert their eggs or young.

There are many different designs for nest boxes, but the most common and often the most effective is a very simple box that can be made from a single plank of wood. By altering the inside dimensions, the size of the hole, and the site where the box is placed, you should be able to attract a variety of different species.

Here are a few basic dimensions for some of the most common cavity nesting species:

Species	Floor Size	Depth	Hole Diameter	Height above ground
Western Bluebird	13x13 cm	20 cm	38 mm	1-3 m (on post or tree)
Chestnut-backed Chickadee	10x10 cm	23 cm	29 mm	1.5-5 m (in tree)
Downy Woodpecker	10x10 cm	23 cm	32 mm	2-6 m (on tree)
Hairy Woodpecker	15x15 cm	35 cm	38 mm	4-6 m (on tree)
House Finch	15x15 cm	15 cm	50 mm	2-4 m (on tree)
House Sparrow	10x10 cm	23 cm	38 mm	1-4 m (on house or tree)
Red-breasted Nuthatch	10x10 cm	23 cm	32 mm	2-6 m (on tree)
Northern Saw-whet Owl	15x15 cm	28 cm	64 mm	4-7 m (on tree)
Western Screech-owl	20x20 cm	35 cm	76 mm	3-10 m (on tree)
European Starling	15x15 cm	40 cm	50 mm	3-8 m (on house or tree)
Violet-green & Tree Swallows	13x13 cm	15 cm	38 mm	3-5 m (on tree or post)
Wood Duck	27x27 cm	60 cm	76 mm	3-7 m (near water)

There are some basic rules to be kept in mind. If the nest box is exposed to full sunlight during the hottest part of the day, the nestlings may die from heat exhaustion, so choose a shaded area, or the northeast side of an exposed tree, post or building. If the box is on a wall, the same will apply — so choose a spot that is shaded by a tree or a climbing plant. Keep the box level or tilted slightly down so that the hole is not exposed to rain. Avoid trees that cats like to climb, or put on an anti-cat barrier at the bottom: an inverted wire cone fixed to the tree about 1 1/2 metres above the ground usually suffices. There is nothing more upsetting than having the family cat bring you a present of the young birds that you have been watching.

Try to put the nest box in a position that looks as natural as possible and emulates a natural cavity. For your own pleasure, situate it where you can see what is going on from some convenient vantage point.

Nest box placement.

A BIRD GARDEN

Food, shelter and water are the necessities for all birds at all seasons. A simple bird feeder will bring a variety of seed-eating birds to the garden, but there is little chance of luring insect-eating birds without an appealing environment for them. Even some of the seed-eating species are very shy at the feeder and to attract these birds it is necessary to "think natural" and create some attractive mini-habitats.

It is possible to determine the types of birds that will come to your garden by providing the sort of surroundings that give them shelter, nesting opportunities and food. Flycatchers and other insect-eating birds will be attracted in spring and summer to flower gardens where insects are likely to be abundant. Seed-eating birds like finches and grosbeaks will find both shelter and food in the wilder sections of a back yard, where shrubs and weeds combine to provide dense cover and year-round access to food in the form of seeds. A varied garden plot will lure birds where a flawless lawn will not, and a mix of shrubs and taller trees will attract a far greater variety and abundance of birds than a hedge of uniform trees or shrubs. It is not only berry bushes and fruit trees that provide food; seeds, insects feeding on plants, and water are at least as likely to entice birds.

Birds are also attracted to gardens where there is plenty of shelter in which to rest during the day, or to roost at night, where

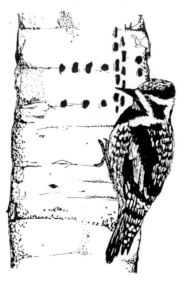

Sapsucker drilling holes on an alder tree trunk for sap.

they can escape from the hottest weather in the summer, and find some protection in the winter. Gardens with mature trees and plenty of shrub cover will be attractive. Some birds also appreciate an area of longer grass and if it is possible to keep an area of the garden as "wild" as you can, it will attract all sorts of creatures, not just birds.

Planting to Attract Birds

Berry Bushes Native shrubs are a principal food source for birds in the wild and will prove a major attraction for birds in the city as well. Although it is possible to transplant shrubs from the wild, this may not be a very conservation-minded practice, unless it is done with care and forethought and with species whose abundance is not an issue. Obviously, if you can get to an area before a developer clears the vegetation, you will not be doing any damage. However, this is not always easy to do and an obvious way to get around the problem is to grow plants from cuttings or seeds. If this does not appeal to you, then try some of the better garden centres, many of which offer a complete range of native shrubs and trees, along with a great deal of good advice.
Among those shrubs that are practical to transplant, and attractive to birds, are blue elderberry and red elderberry, Oregon grape, black twinberry, salal, Indian plum, squashberry, snowberry, thimbleberry, salmonberry, huckleberry, black raspberry, wild rose, flowering currant, gooseberry and blackberry.
Domestic varieties of some of these berry bushes can be obtained from the larger nurseries and garden centres. They may also supply you with a host of other choices in shrubs that birds find equally attractive, including cotoneaster, pyracantha, honeysuckle, raspberry, red and black currant and viburnum.

Trees Fruit trees and bushes sometimes provide an unwelcome attraction to birds, as anyone who grows fruit will know. However, some trees produce fruit that is very attractive to birds, but of little or no value to humans. Trees such as the mountain ash are good berry producers and will be visited by American Robins, Cedar Waxwings and other species. Other trees that grow in this area, such as the arbutus and Garry Oak, are also attractive to birds. Black hawthorn, Pacific crabapple, bitter cherry, cascara and Pacific dogwood are worth planting and cultivating as they may well be visited throughout the winter, or as long as the fruits remain on the trees. Watching the birds search out the fruits will provide you with a good deal of enjoyment.

Starling resting on a fence post.

Water Birds need water throughout the year. A bird bath that is kept unfrozen in the coldest weather will attract many birds. During the summer months, a bird bath can become a busy place. Birds like to bathe more in the summer, and bird baths can provide endless pleasure for both the birds and the birdwatcher.

Choose or build a bird bath that is not too deep (no more than 7 cm), shelves gradually and is finished in a rough texture so that it is easy for birds to grip. Birds get engrossed in drinking and bathing and when they have wet feathers, they don't fly quite so well. Therefore, if the bath is on or near ground level, make sure that it is situated well away from bushes, so that cats can not approach the bath unseen.

You can keep the water in your bird bath unfrozen during the coldest winters with a small heater available on the market, and you can make the bath particularly attractive to birds in summer by creating a trickly flow or spray of water with a small electric pump.

SEASONS OF BIRDWATCHING

Spring

Spring comes early to the west coast with no marked change in seasonal conditions. The first sign of spring is often the increase in the number of ducks on the estuaries and lakes, as birds from the south push north, waiting for the break-up of the ice on their inland breeding sites. The first of the ducks to arrive may be the elegant Northern Pintail, which begin to come north in February. Also arriving in February are the earliest swallows, the Violet-green and Tree Swallows.

This is the time of year when bird-song also begins and many birds that have overwintered suddenly become more noticeable as they begin to establish breeding territories. Some species, such as Great Horned Owls and Western Screech-owls, which are here throughout the year, are best found at this time of the year. Take a walk through one of the forested parks around the city at dusk or before dawn and you may well be rewarded by hearing them.

The increase in bird activity is the prelude to the breeding season and you will notice that many of the birds are actively involved in courtship behaviour. Waterfowl go through many of their breeding displays on the water, and some are very attractive to watch, particularly those of the goldeneyes and Bufflehead. Like the Mallard, the Bufflehead's courtship is far from sedate, with the female frequently being pursued none too gallantly by many males.

Spring is also the time of year when it is easiest to see birds in and around the city. Not only are the numbers and variety of birds swelled by the migrants that are arriving to breed, or passing through on their way to their northern breeding grounds, but the lack of leaves on the deciduous trees makes seeing them much easier. Without doubt, early May is the best time of year to watch for warblers. Later in the year, not only will it be harder to spot them, but the young "look-alike" birds will confuse even the most experienced birder.

Perhaps the most thrilling of the spring sights and sounds, though, are the few skeins of geese that pass high over the city on their flight northward. Canada Geese and occasionally White-fronted and Snow Geese may be seen.

Summer

Summer is the breeding season for most birds and this means a great deal of singing, displaying and nest-building. Once the serious business of incubating the eggs and feeding the young starts, birds become less noticeable and once more secretive. It can be an advantage for a bird to announce its presence when trying to attract a mate or establish a territory, but once eggs are laid and the young hatch, there is a greater need to incubate and feed young birds, and remain undetected by predators.

For those who have put up nest boxes or have the good fortune to have their trees or gardens selected as nesting sites, this time can be great fun. There is something enormously satisfying about witnessing the breeding cycle of birds. From start to finish, it may take a chickadee only about a month to find a mate, build a nest, lay eggs, hatch them and feed their young to the point of fledging. If they happen to use a nest box that you have put up for them, this becomes a very personal experience and the sense of thrill when the young birds fly comes as quite a surprise.

Ducks moult at this time of year and both the male and the females look very much alike for a while. When ducks are moulting, it is known as the "eclipse" plumage; some species can look very different and even the common male Mallard may require more than one look before identification is possible. Birds moult at this time of year to renew their flight feathers before their fall migration, while there is still an abundance of summer food available.

The display posture of a male red-winged blackbird during the mating season.

Autumn

As early as August, birds that have completed their breeding cycle for the year will start migrating south through Victoria and southern Vancouver Island. Birds that breed in the Arctic must complete their breeding as quickly as possible because, by late summer, food sources are already less abundant and colder weather has begun. As young birds fledge, the birds leave their breeding grounds and begin to arrive along our coast. Watch for the increase in numbers of shorebirds and waterfowl now. Estuaries, bays and lakes with muddy shores are particularly good places to visit at this time of year.

Autumn is also the time of year when warblers and many of the other small birds can be frustratingly hard to identify, as the young birds and the moulting adults do not always look the way they ought to according to the books!

Shorter daylight hours and an end to the breeding cycle can often induce some birds — particularly the crows and starlings — to begin their communal roosting behaviour. Each evening large flights of Northwestern Crows stream over the residential areas on their way to safe night roosts on nearby off-shore islands — such as Sidney, James, Chatham and Discovery Islands. Similarly, European Starlings begin to arrive at their night roosts as darkness approaches. Large flocks can be seen in the downtown area as they wheel and circle over their safe havens.

Autumn is the best time to watch out for rarer birds, so be prepared to take a close look at anything that seems odd or unusual. Migrants, especially juveniles, can easily take the wrong turn, and here on the west coast it is possible to get Eurasian birds migrating down the wrong side of the Pacific seaboard. Check every bird in a flock of ducks or shorebirds and look for colours or features that are different from the majority's. Then check your field guide to see if you have found a rarity. If you think you have, call the Victoria Natural History Society's "Rare Bird Alert," (under "Rare" in the telephone directory). Follow the "hot-line" instructions and someone should show up fairly soon to confirm your sighting.

Winter

Here on the west coast, we can look forward to many more species of birds remaining throughout the winter months than is possible in other parts of Canada. The variety of waterfowl and seabirds during the winter can be a source of many hours of fruitful birdwatching. Many bird species overwinter in this coastal area for exactly the same reason that we enjoy living here — the winter temperatures are relatively warm and there is little snow. This means that certain birds do not need to fly south to find a suitable place to over-winter. Birds normally migrate to avoid the harsh weather which makes feeding difficult and birds such as the warblers that rely on a ready source of small insects — which become less available, even in our gentle winters — must leave most Canadian areas.

Early winter is the time of year when feeders work particularly well in attracting birds into the garden. Once you have attracted a few, more will tend to show up and linger on — perhaps even through the winter — because there is safety in numbers. Many birds react swiftly to the danger signals of other species. Although some of the smaller birds will have migrated south, some of the woodland species can be easier to see at this time of year, as there are fewer leaves on the deciduous trees and bushes. Look out for woodpeckers, which always seem more visible in the winter.

This is a good time of year to check your nest boxes, to ensure that they are not broken and to clean them. Put a little dry grass or a few wood shavings in the bottom; this allows air to circulate and helps to make them more attractive to birds in the spring.

KEEPING BIRD NOTES

Now that you have birds coming to the feeder and birds nesting in the bird boxes, why not keep a record of which birds you see in your yard, when, how many and how often? Keeping records is the only way of noting changes and will provide you with many hours of pleasure. A daily or weekly checklist of sightings will tell you a great deal about your avian visitors. It will furnish a record of how numbers change throughout the seasons and from year to year, and of specific migration times of many species. You will soon know just when to expect your first Rufous Hummingbird of the spring, or the first Golden-crowned Sparrow of the autumn.

If you spend time hiking through nearby natural areas or parks, your observations will help you to remember what you saw and when. These observations will tell you what birds were common in which years and what parts of the area were particularly good for various species. As well as being of interest to you, you may be able to make an important contribution to local knowledge by helping ornithologists understand how numbers of birds in your area are changing. This sort of information is often not available when it is needed, and may also help to protect your favorite

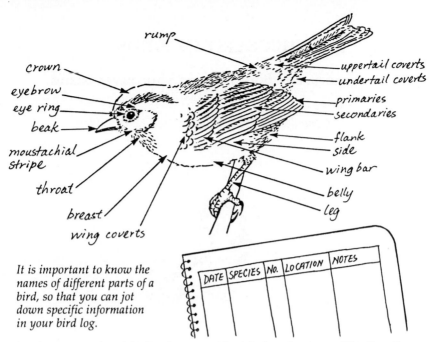

rump

crown

eyebrow
eye ring
beak

moustachial
stripe

throat

breast

wing coverts

uppertail coverts
undertail coverts

primaries
secondaries

flank
side

wing bar

belly

leg

DATE	SPECIES	No.	LOCATION	NOTES

It is important to know the names of different parts of a bird, so that you can jot down specific information in your bird log.

birding spot, should it be threatened with development. The Royal British Columbia Museum and provincial Wildlife Branch appreciate receiving sight-record cards documenting your bird observations, especially those of our less common species.

Keeping good records may allow you to convince the experts that you have seen a particularly rare bird, or may help you describe a problem species to an expert. Try to record a clear image of what the bird looked like — a simple line sketch is ideal, and it really doesn't matter how artistic it is! Include as much information as you can about the bird, its plumage characteristics, its bill, leg colour, sounds, and what behaviour the bird exhibited.

You might also want to keep a bird log. This would include the species you saw, how many, where and when (see diagram).

Keep your records in a notebook to avoid losing them. If you intend to take your notebook on hikes, choose one with a soft waterproof cover; so you can stuff it into a pocket and it will not disintegrate in the rain. A useful tip: pencils write more easily than pens on damp paper.

Another good way to learn more about birds is to join your local natural history or bird society. You will meet many knowledgeable people who will be able to teach you what they know about birds and the best places to see them. Many organizations run field trips to good birdwatching spots and provide the benefit of an expert to help with identification problems.

Good birding!

CHECKLIST OF BIRDS

Victoria and Southeastern Vancouver Island, British Columbia

Compiled by Bryan R. Gates and Keith Taylor

Area covered: South from 49°N latitude at Ladysmith and East from 123°50' W longitude at Ladysmith and Otter Point including the Canadian Gulf Islands and waters to the United States border.

Explanation of Symbols

▬▬▬▬   **Common** - moderate to large numbers in suitable habitats.

————   **Fairly Common** - moderate to low numbers in suitable habitats.

———   **Uncommon** - usually in low numbers or irregular; often local.

- - - - - -   **Rare for this area** - occurs most years but usually few records per year.

•   **Vagrant** - not expected annually but more than 5 records in past century. Outside normal range.

o   **Accidental** - five or fewer records in past century. Far outside normal range.

o→   **Single record** - duration of stay.

(3)   **Number of confirmed records** - accidental species only.

(1)   **Introduced** - survived for 10 years or more.

(E)   **Extirpated** - no longer present in checklist area.

*   **Breeding** - at least one successful nest record for the checklist area.

(OS)   **Offshore** - most likely seen from boat in local marine waters.

(FV)   **Further Verification Required** - records not well documented or unconfirmed by second observer.

(L)   **Local** - may be fairly common but confined to localized sites.

Common Name	Code	Nesting	Jan	Feb	Mar	Apr	May	Jun	Jul	Aug	Sep	Oct	Nov	Dec
......Red-throated Loon	RTLO													
......Pacific Loon	PALO													
......Common Loon	COLO	★												
......Yellow-billed Loon	YBLO													
......Pied-billed Grebe	PBGR	★												
......Horned Grebe	HOGR													
......Red-necked Grebe	RNGR													
......Eared Grebe	EAGR													
......Western Grebe	WEGR													
......Clark's Grebe	CLGR						•				•	•	•••	
......Short-tailed Albatross (1)	STAL								○					
......Northern Fulmar (OS)	NOFU													
......Pink-footed Shearwater (OS, 2, FV)	PFSH								○		○			
......Sooty Shearwater (OS)	SOSH													
......Short-tailed Shearwater (OS)	STSH													
......Black-vented Shearwater (OS, 3)	BVSH			○							○	○		
......Fork-tailed Storm-Petrel (OS)	FTSP													
......Leach's Storm-Petrel (OS)	LESP													
......American White Pelican	AWPE						•••			•••				
......Brown Pelican (OS)	BRPE													
......Double-crested Cormorant	DCCO	★												
......Brandt's Cormorant	BRCO	★												
......Pelagic Cormorant	PECO	★												
......Frigatebird sp. (1, FV)			○											
......American Bittern	AMBI													
......Great Blue Heron	GBHE	★												
......Great Egret	GREG						••			•	•	••	•	
......Snowy Egret (3)	SNEG							○		○			○	
......Cattle Egret	CAEG													
......Green-backed Heron	GRHE	★												
......Black-crowned Night-Heron (4)	BCNH						○ ○●○ → ○○			○				

132

Common Name	Code	Nesting	Jan	Feb	Mar	Apr	May	Jun	Jul	Aug	Sep	Oct	Nov	Dec
......White-faced Ibis	WFIB						o		o					
......Tundra Swan	TUSW													
......Trumpeter Swan	TRUS													
......Mute Swan (I)	MUSW	★												
......Greater White-fronted Goose	GWFG													
......Snow Goose	SNGO													
......Emperor Goose	EMGO		•	•	•	••							•	•
......Brant	BRAN													
......Canada Goose	CAGO	★												
......Wood Duck	WODU	★												
......Green-winged Teal	GWTE	★												
......American Black Duck (I)	ABDU													
......Mallard	MALL	★												
......Northern Pintail	NOPI													
......Blue-winged Teal	BWTE	★												
......Cinnamon Teal	CITE	★												
......Northern Shoveler	NOSL	★												
......Gadwall	GADW													
......Eurasian Wigeon	EUWI													
......American Wigeon	AMWI	★												
......Canvasback	CANV													
......Redhead	REDH													
......Ring-necked Duck	RNDU													
......Tufted Duck	TUDU			•	•	•							•	•
......Greater Scaup	GRSC													
......Lesser Scaup	LESC													
......King Eider (I)	KIEI		o											
......Steller's Eider (I)	STEI			o→										
......Harlequin Duck	HADU													
......Oldsquaw	OLDS													
......Black Scoter	BLSC													
......Surf Scoter	SUSC													
......White-winged Scoter	WWSC													
......Common Goldeneye	COGO	★												
......Barrow's Goldeneye	BAGO													
......Bufflehead	BUFF	★												
......Hooded Merganser	HOME	★												
......Common Merganser	COME	★												
......Red-breasted Merganser	RBME													
......Ruddy Duck	RUDU	★												
......Turkey Vulture	TUVU	★												

Common Name	Code	Nesting	Jan	Feb	Mar	Apr	May	Jun	Jul	Aug	Sep	Oct	Nov	Dec
......Osprey	OSPR	★												
......Bald Eagle	BAEA	★												
......Northern Harrier	NOHA													
......Sharp-shinned Hawk	SSHA													
......Cooper's Hawk	COHA	★												
......Northern Goshawk	NOGO	★												
......Swainson's Hawk	SWHA													
......Red-tailed Hawk	RTHA	★												
......Rough-legged Hawk	RLHA													
......Golden Eagle	GOEA	★												
......American Kestrel	AMKE	★												
......Merlin	MERL	★												
......Peregrine Falcon	PEFA	★												
......Gyrfalcon	GYRF													
......Prairie Falcon (2, FV)	PRFA													
......Gray Partridge (I,E)	GRPA	★												
......Ring-necked Pheasant	RNPH	★												
......Blue Grouse	BLGR	★												
......Ruffed Grouse	RUGR	★												
......California Quail	CAQU	★												
......Mountain Quail	MOQU	★												
......Virginia Rail	VIRA	★												
......Sora	SORA	★												
......American Coot	AMCO	★												
......Sandhill Crane	SACR													
......Black-bellied Plover	BBPL													
......Lesser Golden-Plover	LGPL													
......dominica race														
......fulva race														
......Semipalmated Plover	SEPL													
......Killdeer	KILL	★												
......Black Oystercatcher	BLOY	★												
......Black-necked Stilt (3)	BNST													
......American Avocet (3)	AMAV													
......Greater Yellowlegs	GRYE													
......Lesser Yellowlegs	LEYE													
......Solitary Sandpiper	SOSA													
......Willet	WILL													

Common Name	Code	Nesting	Jan	Feb	Mar	Apr	May	Jun	Jul	Aug	Sep	Oct	Nov	Dec
......Wandering Tattler	WATA												
......Spotted Sandpiper	SDSA	*											
......Terek Sandpiper (1)	TESA												
......Upland Sandpiper	UPSA												
......Whimbrel	WHIM												
......Long-billed Curlew (3)	LBCU												
......Hudsonian Godwit (3)	HUGO												
......Bar-tailed Godwit (4)	BTGO												
......Marbled Godwit	MAGO												
......Ruddy Turnstone	RUTU												
......Black Turnstone	BLTU												
......Surfbird	SURF												
......Red Knot	REKN												
......Sanderling	SAND												
......Semipalmated Sandpiper	SESA												
......Western Sandpiper	WESA												
......Least Sandpiper	LESA												
......White-rumped Sandpiper (3, FV)	WRSA												
......Baird's Sandpiper	BASA												
......Pectoral Sandpiper	PESA												
......Sharp-tailed Sandpiper	SHSA												
......Rock Sandpiper	ROSA												
....Dunlin	DUNL												
......Curlew Sandpiper (1)	CUSA												
......Stilt Sandpiper	STSA												
......Buff-breased Sandpiper	BBSA												
......Ruff	RUFF												
......Short-billed Dowitcher	SBDO												
......Long-billed Dowitcher	LBDO												
......Common Snipe	COSN	*											
......Wilson's Phalarope	WIPH	*											
......Red-necked Phalarope	RNPL												
......Red Phalarope	REPH												
......Pomarine Jaeger	POJA												
......Parasitic Jaeger	PAJA												
......Long-tailed Jaeger	LTJA												
......South Polar Skua (6)	SPSK												
......Franklin's Gull	FRGU												
......Little Gull	LIGU												
......Common Black-headed Gull	CBHG												
......Bonaparte's Gull	BOGU												
......Heermann's Gull	HMGU												

135

Common Name	Code	Nesting	Jan	Feb	Mar	Apr	May	Jun	Jul	Aug	Sep	Oct	Nov	Dec
.....Mew Gull	MEGU													
.....Ring-billed Gull	RBGU													
.....California Gull	CAGU													
.....Herring Gull	HEGU													
.....Thayer's Gull	THGU													
.....Slaty-backed Gull (1)	SBGU													
.....Western Gull	WEGU													
.....Glaucous-winged Gull	GWGU	★												
.....Glaucous Gull	GLGU													
.....Black-legged Kittiwake	BLKI													
.....Ross' Gull (1)	ROGU													
.....Sabine's Gull	SAGU													
.....Caspian Tern	CATE													
.....Elegant Tern (3)	ELTE													
.....Common Tern	CMTE													
.....Arctic Tern	ARTE													
.....Forster's Tern (2)	FOTE													
.....Black Tern (2, FV)	BLTE													
.....Common Murre	COMU													
.....Pigeon Guillemot	PIGU	★												
.....Marbled Murrelet	MAMU													
.....Kittlitz's Murrelet (1)	KIMU													
.....Ancient Murrelet	ANMU													
.....Cassin's Auklet	CAAU													
.....Rhinoceros Auklet	RHAU	★												
.....Tufted Puffin	TUPU	★												
.....Horned Puffin (4)	HOPU													
.....Rock Dove	RODO	★												
.....Band-tailed Pigeon	BTPI	★												
.....Mourning Dove	MODO	★												
.....Yellow-billed Cuckoo (3, E)	YBCU													
.....Common Barn-Owl	CBOW	★												
.....Western Screech-Owl	WSOW	★												
.....Great Horned Owl	GHOW	★												
.....Snowy Owl	SNOW													
.....Northern Hawk-Owl (2)	NHOW													
.....Northern Pygmy-Owl	NPOW	★												
.....Burrowing Owl (5)	BUOW													
.....Barred Owl	BAOW	★												
.....Great Grey Owl (1)	GGOW													

Common Name	Code	Nesting	Jan	Feb	Mar	Apr	May	Jun	Jul	Aug	Sep	Oct	Nov	Dec
......Long-eared Owl	LEOW		●●		●	●							●	●●●●
......Short-eared Owl	SEOW		--	--		-					---	--	--	--
......Northern Saw-whet Owl	NSWO	★	---	---	---	---	---	---	---	---	---	---	---	---
......Common Nighthawk	CONI	★						▬▬▬						
......Common Poorwill (1)	COPO							○						
......Black Swift	BLSW						-- ▬	--						
......Vaux's Swift	VASW	★					-▬			▬				
......Anna's Hummingbird	ANHU	★												
......Costa's Hummingbird (1)	COHU						○							
......Rufous Hummingbird	RUHU	★				-- ▬▬▬▬▬▬ --								
......Belted Kingfisher	BEKI	★	▬▬▬▬▬▬▬▬▬▬▬▬▬▬▬▬▬▬▬▬▬▬▬▬											
......Lewis' Woodpecker	LEWO	★	-		-	---	---			---	---			
......Yellow-bellied Sapsucker (1)	YBSA													○
......Red-naped Sapsucker	RNSA					●●●●●●				●●●●●● ●				
......Red-breasted Sapsucker	RBSA	★												
......Downy Woodpecker	DOWO	★	▬▬▬▬▬▬▬▬▬▬▬▬▬▬▬▬▬▬▬▬▬▬▬▬											
......Hairy Woodpecker	HAWO	★	▬▬▬▬▬▬▬▬▬▬▬▬▬▬▬▬▬▬▬▬▬▬▬▬											
......Northern Flicker	NOFL	★	▬▬▬▬▬▬▬▬▬▬▬▬▬▬▬▬▬▬▬▬▬▬▬▬											
......Pileated Woodpecker	PIWO	★	▬▬▬▬▬▬▬▬▬▬▬▬▬▬▬▬▬▬▬▬▬▬▬▬											
......Olive-sided Flycatcher	OSFL	★					▬▬▬▬▬ --							
......Western Wood-Pewee	WWPE	★					▬▬▬▬ --							
......Willow Flycatcher	WIFL	★					▬▬ --							
......Least Flycatcher (5)	LEFL	★					○○○							
......Hammond's Flycatcher	HAFL	★				-- ▬▬▬▬▬ --								
......Western Flycatcher	WEFL	★				-- ▬▬▬▬▬▬▬▬							
......Say's Phoebe	SAPH		●●●●		●		●●		●●					
......Tropical Kingbird (4)	TRKI										○○○			
......Western Kingbird	WEKI					---------								
......Eastern Kingbird	EAKI						-----------							
......Scissor-tailed Flycatcher (2)	STFL						○				○			
......Eurasian Skylark	EUSY	★	▬▬▬▬▬▬▬▬▬▬▬▬▬▬▬▬▬▬▬▬▬▬▬▬											
......Horned Lark	HOLA	★	--------------------								▬	--		
......Purple Martin	PUMA	★					--		--					
......Tree Swallow	TRSW	★			-- ▬▬▬▬▬▬▬									

Common Name	Code	Nesting	Jan	Feb	Mar	Apr	May	Jun	Jul	Aug	Sep	Oct	Nov	Dec
......Violet-green Swallow	VGSW	★		–	–	▬	▬	▬	▬					
......Northern Rough-winged Swallow	NRWS	★			–	▬	▬	▬	▬	–				
......Bank Swallow	BKSW			–	–		–	–	–					
......Cliff Swallow	CLSW	★			–	▬	▬	▬	▬			–		
......Barn Swallow	BASW	★			–	▬	▬	▬	▬	▬	▬			
......Gray Jay	GRJA	★												
......Steller's Jay	STJA	★	▬	▬	▬	▬	▬	▬	▬	▬	▬	▬	▬	▬
......Blue Jay	BLJA		●	●	●	●	●	●		●		●	●	●
......Clark's Nutcracker	CLNU									●	● ● ● ●			
......Black-billed Magpie (5)	BBMA			○ ○							○		○	○
......Northwestern Crow	NOCR	★												
......Common Raven	CORA	★												
......Chestnut-backed Chickadee	CBCH	★	▬	▬	▬	▬	▬	▬	▬	▬	▬	▬	▬	▬
......Bushtit	BUSH	★	▬	▬	▬	▬	▬	▬	▬	▬	▬	▬	▬	▬
......Red-breasted Nuthatch	RBNU	★	▬	▬	▬	▬	▬	▬	▬	▬	▬	▬	▬	▬
......White-breasted Nuthatch (3)	WBNU		○→		→							○	○	
......Pygmy Nuthatch (FV)	PYNU								○					
......Brown Creeper	BRCR	★	▬	▬	▬	▬	▬	▬	▬	▬	▬	▬	▬	▬
......Rock Wren	ROWR	★	●				●	●	●	● ●	●	●		
......Bewick's Wren	BEWR	★	▬	▬	▬									
......House Wren	HOWR	★				▬	▬	▬	▬	–	–	–		
......Winter Wren	WIWR	★	▬	▬	▬									
......Marsh Wren	MAWR	★												
......American Dipper	AMDI	★			–									
......Golden-crowned Kinglet	GCKI	★	▬	▬	▬					▬	▬	▬	▬	▬
......Ruby-crowned Kinglet	RCKI		▬	▬	▬	–	–	–			–	▬	▬	▬
......Blue-gray Gnatcatcher (1)	BGGN											○		
......Northern Wheatear (1)	NOWH											○		
......Western Bluebird	WEBL	★												
......Mountain Bluebird	MOBL				– –	–					– –	–		
......Townsend's Solitaire	TOSO	★			–									
......Veery (1)	VEER							○						
......Swainson's Thrush	SWTH	★			–	–	▬	▬	▬	▬	–	–		

138

Common Name	Code	Nesting	Jan	Feb	Mar	Apr	May	Jun	Jul	Aug	Sep	Oct	Nov	Dec
......Hermit Thrush	HETH													
......American Robin	AMRO	★												
......Varied Thrush	VATH	★												
......Northern Mockingbird	NOMO	★												
......Wagtail sp. (1, FV)							o							
......Water Pipit	WAPI													
......Bohemian Waxwing	BOWA													
......Cedar Waxwing	CEWA	★												
......Northern Shrike	NOSH													
......European Starling	EUST	★												
......Crested Myna (I, E)	CRMY		o o	o	o									
......Solitary Vireo	SOVI	★												
......Hutton's Vireo	HUVI	★												
......Warbling Vireo	WAVI	★												
......Red-eyed Vireo	REVI	★												
......Orange-crowned Warbler	OCWA	★												
......Nashville Warbler	NAWA					• • •			• • •	• • •	• •			
......Yellow Warbler	YEWA	★												
......Magnolia Warbler (1)	MAWA							o						
......Yellow-rumped Warbler	YRWA	★												
Black-throated Gray Warbler	BTGW	★												
......Townsend's Warbler	TOWA	★												
......Palm Warbler	PAWA													
......Blackpoll Warbler (1)	BPWA						o							
......Northern Waterthrush (4)	NOWA						o			o o				
......MacGillivray's Warbler	MGWA	★												
......Common Yellowthroat	COYE	★												
......Wilson's Warbler	WIWA	★												
......Rose-breasted Grosbeak (2)	RBGR							o o						
......Black-headed Grosbeak	BHGR	★												
......Lazuli Bunting	LZBU						• • • • •							
......Dickcissel (2)	DICK		→									o	o →	
......Rufous-sided Towhee	RSTO	★												
......American Tree Sparrow	ATSP		• • • • • •									• • • • •	
......Chipping Sparrow	CHSP	★												
......Western Tanager	WETA	★												

Common Name	Code	Nesting	Jan	Feb	Mar	Apr	May	Jun	Jul	Aug	Sep	Oct	Nov	Dec
......Brewer's Sparrow (1)	BRSP						○							
......Vesper Sparrow (L)	VESP	★												
......Lark Sparrow	LASP		•		•	•	•					•	•	•
......Lark Bunting (1)	LABU						○							
......Savannah Sparrow	SAVS	★												
......Grasshopper Sparrow (1)	GRSP											○		
......Fox Sparrow	FOSP													
......Song Sparrow	SOSP	★												
......Lincoln's Sparrow	LISP													
......Swamp Sparrow	SWSP		•	•	•	•	•	•				•	•	•
......White-throated Sparrow	WTSP													
......Golden-crowned Sparrow	GCSP	★												
......White-crowned Sparrow	WCSP	★												
......Harris' Sparrow	HASP													
......Dark-eyed Junco	DEJU	★												
......Lapland Longspur	LALO													
......Chestnut-collared Longspur (2)	CCLO						○				○			
......Snow Bunting	SNBU													
......Bobolink	BOBO							•			•	• • • •		
......Red-winged Blackbird	RWBL	★												
......Western Meadowlark	WEME	★												
......Yellow-headed Blackbird	YHBL													
......Rusty Blackbird	RUBL													
......Brewer's Blackbird	BRBL	★												
......Common Grackle (3)	COGR		○→								○	○→		
......Brown-headed Cowbird	BHCO	★												
......Northern Oriole	NOOR	★												
......Brambling (1)	BRAM											○		
......Rosy Finch	ROFI		•									• • • • •		
......Pine Grosbeak	PIGR													
......Purple Finch	PUFI	★												
......House Finch	HOFI	★												
......Red Crossbill	RECR	★												
......White-winged Crossbill (5)	WWCR		○				○ ○							○ ○
......Common Redpoll (5)	CORE		○ ○											○ ○
......Pine Siskin	PISI	★												
......American Goldfinch	AMGO	★												
......Evening Grosbeak	EVGR	★												
......House Sparrow (I)	HOSP	★												

Total 331 Species

RECOMMENDED READING

There are many excellent books on the market, among the most useful and informative being the following:

Attracting and Feeding Birds in British Columbia. R. Wayne Campbell and Harold Hosford. British Columbia Provincial Museum. Methods Manual Number 7, Victoria.

Attracting Backyard Wildlife - A Guide for Nature Lovers. Bill Merilees. Whitecap Books, Toronto.

The Audubon Society Master Guide to Birding. 3 Volumes. Alfred A. Knopf, New York.

A Bibliography of British Columbia Ornithology. R. Wayne Campbell, Harry R. Carter, Christopher D. Shepard & Charles J. Guiguet. British Columbia Provincial Museum. 1979.

A Bibliography of British Columbia Ornithology, Volume 2. R. Wayne Campbell, Tracey D. Hooper & Neil K. Dawe. Royal British Columbia Museum. 1988.

The Bird Feeder Book. Donald and Lillian Stokes. Little Brown and Company. 1987.

The Birdfinding Guide to Canada. J. Cam Finlay. Hurtig Publishers. 1984.

Birds of British Columbia. C. J. Guiguet. British Columbia Provincial Museum.

1 The Woodpeckers. 2 The Crows and their Allies. Handbook #6. 1954.

Alien Animals in British Columbia. Handbook #14. 1957.

Chickadees, Thrushes, Kinglets, Pipits, Waxwings and Shrikes. Handbook #22. 1964.

Diving Birds and Tube-nosed Swimmers. Handbook #29. 1971.

Gulls, Terns, Jaegers and Skua. Handbook #13. 1971.

The Owls. Handbook #18. 1970.

The Shorebirds. Handbook #8. 1962.

Upland Gamebirds. Handbook #10. 1970.

Waterfowl. Handbook #15. 1971.

Birds of British Columbia: Nonpasserines - Loons through Woodpeckers. R. Wayne Campbell, Neil K. Dawe, Ian McTaggart-Cowan, John M.Cooper, Gary W. Kaiser and Michael C. E. McNall. Royal British Columbia Museum, Victoria. Available late 1989.

Birds of Canada. Revised Edition. W. Earl Godfrey. National Museum of Natural Sciences. 1986.

Birds of North America: A Guide to Field Identification. Chandler S. Robbins, Bertel Bruun & Herbert S. Zim. Golden Press, Western Publishing Inc.. 1983.

Complete Book of Birdhouse Construction for Woodworkers. Scott D. Campbell. Dover Publications, Inc. 1984.

Field Guide to the Birds of North America. S. L. Scott (editor). National Geographic Society. 1983.

Field Guide to Western Birds. R. T. Peterson. Houghton Mifflin. New Edition: 1989.

The Naturalist's Guide to the Victoria Region. Edited with contributions by Jim Wenton and David Stirling. Victoria Natural History Society. 1986.

Trees, Shrubs and Flowers to Know in British Columbia. C. P. Lyons. J. M. Dent & Sons (Canada) Limited. 1976.

Victoria in a Knapsack, a Guide to the Natural Areas of Southern Vancouver Island. Sierra Club of British Columbia. 1985.

The Victoria Naturalist. The Victoria Natural History Society, Victoria. (Published six times a year.)

Where to Find Birds in British Columbia. Second edition. David M. Mark. Kestrel Press. 1984.

DIRECTORY OF ORGANIZATIONS

Arrowsmith Natural History Society
Box 1542
Parksville, B.C. V0R 2S0

Comox-Strathcona Naturalists
Box 3222
Courtenay, B.C. V9N 5N4

Cowichan Valley Naturalists
Box 361
Duncan, B.C. V9L 3X5

Mitlenatch Field Naturalists
Box 392
Campbell River, B.C. V8W 5B6

Naniamo Field Naturalists
Box 125
Naniamo, B.C. V9R 5K4

Pender Island Field Naturalists
c/o Ron McLardy
RR #1
Pender Island, B.C. V0N 2M0

Salt Spring Trail and Nature Club
Box 998
Ganges, B.C. V0S 1E0

Victoria Natural History Society
Box 5220
Victoria, B.C. V8R 6N4

INDEX TO BIRDS

ABOUT THE AUTHORS

Robin Bovey is a writer and photographer living in western Canada. He worked for a variety of environmental agencies in Britain before moving to Canada. In 1988, he co-authored and did the photography for *Mosses Lichens and Ferns of Northwest North America*. He is the author of *Birds of Edmonton* and *Birds of Calgary* and is a keen birdwatcher.

R. Wayne Campbell has written more than 300 scientific and popular articles on the birds and other vertebrates of British Columbia. He is the lead author of *Birds of British Columbia* (Volume I, 1989), which is an analysis of over a million specimen, sight and breeding records of birds in the province. He is an Elected and Life Member of the American Ornithologists' Union and is a Registered Professional Biologist.

Bryan R. Gates is a Registered Professional Biologist who has had more than 25 years of experience in wildlife management and environmental planning. He devotes a great deal of his time to ornithology and to the conservation and study of British Columbia's natural resources. He leads the birders' group of the Victoria Natural History Society and is Past President of the Association of Professional Biologists of B.C.

ABOUT THE ILLUSTRATORS

Lead illustrator Ewa Pluciennik, who specializes in water colour and oil paintings, was born and raised in Opole, Silesia, Poland where she received her artistic training. She has been living in Canada for nearly five years.

Contributing illustrators Kitty Ho and Donna McKinnon are freelance artists living in Alberta. Joan Johnston lives in British Columbia.